Praise for

Love Letters from Janey

"Janey Cheu was a lady with spunk, determination, and the ability to care about herself and those around her. She moved between Chinese and American cultures at a time when there was a large divide between them. She honored both cultures, got an education, married and raised a family, and was not afraid to take a leading role in her work environment. It is because of women like her that our world has evolved to the point that it has. This is an excellent read and I highly recommend it."

— ***Bonnie Cehovet***, *writer/editor, BonnieCehovet.com*

"A very wholesome and heartwarming read that puts us in the shoes of a Chinese American couple in 1960s San Francisco Chinatown. Definitely a unique story that many can relate to from that time and beyond as we follow the couple as they learn to navigate the real world of love, school, work, and family."

— ***Kimberly Szeto***, *Programs Coordinator, Chinese Historical Society of America*

"By keeping all the letters he received from Janey, Richard proved that he deeply cared for his wife. A true love story for a husband, a lover, a friend, and a family member. Highly recommended for people who want to learn what true love is."

— ***Nancy Yu Law***, *Director, Chinatown History & Culture Association*

"Sharing a profound love and understanding is an extraordinary experience at any age. Richard Cheu's sensitive compilation of love letters from his remarkable wife, Janey Young Cheu, describes 55 years of her intimate experience at the Stanford University "finishing school" in the 1960s, traversing her stellar professional career as a microbiologist and Ed.D., while raising three sons and passionately supporting her husband. This insightful, finely tuned, and exquisitely written collection chronicles the life of this superbly talented yet unassuming Chinese American woman as she overcomes societal discrimination and family limitations. This assemblage portrays her deep humanity and genuine sensitivity to her family, her culture, and the many facets of her complex world she lovingly embraced."

— ***Nancy Blieden***, *Ph.D., psychoanalyst, American Psychoanalytic Association*

Love Letters From Janey

Love Letters From Janey

50 Years
of Breaking Barriers
Together

Richard Cheu

CheuWrites
cheuwrites.com

CONTENTS

Foreword

"Life as an American-born Chinese in the decades after World War II was one continuous anti-Asian incident," writes Richard Cheu. Few writings capture the milieu of growing up in this environment better than *Love Letters from Janey: 50 Years of Breaking Barriers Together*, a testimony to love, perseverance, and changing social norms. This book's 167 letters from Chinese American woman Janey Mildred Young serve as both a tribute to her life and love and a portrait in courage as Janey confronts the turbulence of an America making its way through racism and women's rights issues.

Why is Janey's story particularly and uniquely revealing? Because, as her husband Richard writes, "The generation of Chinese Americans to which Janey's and my parents belonged established a beachhead in the struggle to obtain civil and legal rights for all Asian Americans. Most of them, except for the very rich or corrupt, were thwarted in their efforts to achieve economic or professional success in a white society." Richard Cheu provides an equally fine tribute to his wife in a preface that reviews her life during these times and her many achievements against all odds: "Janey proved that Betty Friedan was right. Over the next five decades, she was a curriculum developer and systems engineer at Bell Laboratories, one of the first two women and the only Asian American woman to receive the highest technical award at that company, and associate director of the Institute for Science, Technology, and Social Education at Rutgers University."

Richard's words continue throughout these letters from Janey, adding social and political perspective to the writings between them that consider their differences, draw new connections, and reflect hopes, aspirations, and fear as their love grows. Janey writes of the honesty between them, "The other day a friend of mine gave me some very acute objective criticisms of myself. It certainly made me stop and think and try some quick reevaluations. It all seemed to boil down to my trying to live up to a certain idealist image, sort of how I think I should be or living up to a certain character I want others to see in me. I guess this is what you term a 'façade.' Needless to say, when one trusts another, it is so much easier to be honest and sincere. So I guess it is because I trust you so completely that I can be completely uninhibited and truly honest."

While Janey's writings alone would have been compelling, it is husband Richard who places her letters in the perspective of their times and the events that affected not just them and their families, but the Chinese community and culture in America. This juxtaposition of emotional letters reflecting on religion, wealth, values, and growing love provides the foundation of experiences, but it is the blend of Richard's astute commentary and Janey's exuberant reflections that give this book its special depth and atmosphere. Without either one, the result would be singular. Together, this book is a masterful reflection on Asian American experience, culture, changing times, and how one couple navigates these family and societal forces to build a life both individually as professionals and together.

D. Donovan
Senior Reviewer
Midwest Book Review

Preface

Janey Mildred Young was born in Los Angeles in 1938. Her parents, John Chew Young and Mary Lee Young, were American-born Chinese, as was her grandfather, Yoke Suey Lee. Her grandfather was born in San Francisco and worked with his father in the San Francisco Chinatown merchant firm of Quong Shing Lung, which served as the American agent for merchant firms in China. Yoke Suey Lee subsequently moved his wife and children to Shanghai. He died in 1922 aboard a ship bound for China. His widow, Shee Wong (Janey Young's grandmother), returned to San Francisco with her children in 1924. She was detained at the Angel Island Immigration Station in San Francisco Bay under the terms of the Chinese Exclusion Act of 1882, which prevented Chinese laborers from immigrating to the United States. She was separated from her children for 16 months before an immigration lawyer was able to gain her release and reunion with her children. During this interim, Mary Lee—Janey's mother— was the children's surrogate mother.

Janey's father was raised in San Jose, California's second Chinatown—the first was destroyed by arson in 1887—where his father was a merchant. John Chew Young graduated from Stanford University in 1937 with a degree in petroleum engineering and was hired by Standard Oil of California. John and Mary moved to Whittier, California, before Janey was born. John's parents joined the Whittier household a few years later and Janey fondly remembered Grandpa relishing his morning doughnut. One thing John Young did not relish was avocados. The nation had not fully recovered from the Great Depression when he graduated from Stanford. Having a job in the petroleum industry was a sign of good fortune, but money was tight in

13

the Young household. There was an avocado tree in the backyard of the rented home and Janey remembered that her mother made her father an avocado sandwich for his lunch every day to save money.

John loved horseback riding and he joined the Stanford ROTC for the specific purpose of riding horses for free in addition to the army paying his tuition. Upon his graduation from Stanford he was commissioned as a second lieutenant in the United States Army. In 1942 he was activated by the army with the rank of captain and served three years in the China-Burma-India combat theater. While he was on active duty, there were still five mouths to feed in Whittier, Connie was born in 1941 and John's parents also joined the household. Mary, reflecting her father's merchant proclivity, opened a gift shop and catered to the numerous retired missionaries living in Whittier—especially those who had served in China. Janey said the missionaries would talk about their household as "that cute Chinese family." Mary could not manage all the details of operating a gift shop so she recruited a volunteer, six-year-old Janey. In a sense, Janey didn't have an ordinary childhood and was given adult responsibilities while still a child. She was tasked with gift shop duties ordinarily assigned to someone much older. Decades later she vividly remembered being at the San Francisco train station by herself, waiting for her mother to return, and watching over the merchandise purchased in Chinatown to be taken to Whittier via Los Angeles. Her self-confidence was on display when she, her mother, and grandmother were traveling across the United States on a wartime troop train. Grandma was a fearsome figure for her grandchildren. In Chicago, she said something that irritated Janey and Janey shot back, "If you don't listen to me I'll lose you." Grandma listened. On another occasion, reflecting the atmosphere of World War II, Janey told her grandma, "You bomb, you fix. Me bomb, me fix."

Having her husband in combat for three years and not knowing if he would come home alive was extremely stressful for Mary. The stress was heightened by a letter from one of John's translators telling Mary that John was being rotated back to the United States. Unfortunately, the translator described in detail a recent battle in which the Japanese soldiers refused to surrender, which only worsened Mary's concerns and brought back memories of the time when a troop train arrived in the Oakland depot, all the troops disembarked, and John was not among them. The train had stopped outside the station momentarily. John, as the senior officer on the train, got off to see what the problem was and then the train moved off into the station without him. Much later, he trudged into the station, to Mary's great relief.

Imported soy sauce from China had been unavailable during the war and the situation didn't improve with the takeover of China by the Communists in 1949. John joined his brother-in-law, George, in 1942 to establish a soy sauce factory in San Francisco. Mary contributed a significant portion of the financing to make possible their dream of establishing the company near Chinatown. John moved the family to San Francisco, where Janey experienced racism firsthand in the city's segregated Chinatown. She attend the segregated elementary school for "oriental children," Commodore Stockton. She claimed that I, in my traffic boy duties, accosted her one day for walking through the school yard without a pass and made her cry. I have no memory of such an incident, but it is an example of her excellent memory.

Life as an American-born Chinese in the decades after World War II was one continuous anti-Asian incident. John wanted to move the family to San Francisco's newly developed Richmond District, which was off-limits for nonwhite residents. At John's memorial service at the army's Presidio in San Francisco, his white fellow officer told of buying the house John wanted and reselling it to him. John's goal was to move to a school district that was not de facto segregated. The usual educational journey for Chinese American students living in Chinatown was from Commodore Stockton Elementary School to Francisco Junior High, and then Galileo High School. At each school, the white teachers struggled to teach the mostly recently arrived immigrant and first-generation Chinese children the skills of a basic education, including English. Many of the students developed an accented and grammatically incorrect Chinatown English dialect because the language spoken at home was Cantonese. The dialect immediately identified them as Chinese residents and was an economic disadvantage in applying for work outside Chinatown. The move to the Richmond District allowed Janey and subsequently her siblings to attend George Washington High School, which was within walking distance from their new home. Living in a white neighborhood and attending a diversified high school did not mean escaping racism. San Francisco was the epicenter of the anti-Chinese movement in the 1870s that fomented the passage of the 1882 Chinese Exclusion Act and subsequent legislation. Exclusion of Asian immigrants in the United States did not end until 1968.

The economic and social strictures of racism were uppermost in the minds of Chinese Americans during the years of Janey's youth. Our parents unfailingly reminded us, "If you want to win a job, you have to be twice as good as the white people competing for the same position." There was a consensus in the Chinese American community that the three safest and most respectable occupations were medical doctor, engineer, and professor. The focus was on practicality—a decent income. The least respected professions were in the arts: musician, actor, or performer. As a teenager, my dream was to be a flutist in a symphony orchestra. I played a flute solo at my high school graduation. However, my parents strongly discouraged the idea of my attempting to be a professional musician. My music teacher, Howard Fast, taught me a great deal about life but not so much about musicianship because he knew that to be a musician in a professional symphony you had to be a white male. (The ultra-conservative Vienna Philharmonic didn't accept women until 1997 because the all-male orchestra members claimed that women musicians would lower the orchestra's standard of performance.)

Chinese American communities in the United States have necessarily been conservative enclaves of safety and mutual support since the arrival of two waves of Chinese sojourners in the 19th century. Chinese gold prospectors came to the United States as free men responding to the discovery of gold in California in 1848. In the mid-1860s, when the Central Pacific Railroad was unable to hire enough white laborers to construct the western portion of the Transcontinental Railroad, it finally resorted to hiring laborers from China through Chinese agents. The majority returned home to China after completing their contracts, while others stayed to build more railroads in the West. They were not coolies, as claimed by American racists. Coolies were indigent men from China and India who were sent to the Caribbean and South America as slave replacements. The hue and cry of Americans against the Chinese was "They're taking our gold and our jobs." San Francisco's Chinatown in the 19th century was a Chinese merchant and trading enclave that also provided essential amenities for transient and resident Chinese, such as banking, food, shelter, entertainment, and, most importantly, safety from attack by whites. In her book *Driven Out: The Forgotten War Against Chinese Americans*, Jean Phaelzer cites more than 200 instances of violence and expulsion in the American West directed specifically at Chinese Americans between 1849 and 1905. In Tacoma, Washington, an armed mob drove out all the Chinese residents and then burned the city's Chinatown to the ground. San Jose was also obliterated by arson. On October 24, 1871, a white mob descended on Los Angeles's Chinatown and committed the largest and most violent racial attack on Chinese in the city's history, an incident known as the Chinese Massacre of 1871. Seventeen Chinese were lynched and two others died from their wounds. San Francisco's corrupt administration provided minimal municipal services and left Chinatown to manage itself. In 1905, the mayor informed the Public Health Department that the extensive tuberculosis problem in Chinatown was for the Chinese to solve and not a municipal matter. Tuberculosis in Chinatown was not brought under control until the 1960s, long after the effective treatment of tuberculosis with antibiotics was developed in 1949.

The generation of Chinese Americans to which Janey's and my parents belonged established a beachhead in the struggle to obtain civil and legal rights for all Asian Americans. Most of them, except for the very rich or corrupt, were thwarted in their efforts to achieve economic or professional success in a white society. John Young complained that his managers claimed his engineering work as theirs. My father, a graduate of Stanford Medical School, never received privileges to practice in any of San Francisco's private hospitals. His practice was limited to treating Chinese residents of San Francisco's Chinatown.

After graduating from high school, Janey entered Stanford University, where racism was as prevalent as it was in San Francisco. In addition to the socioeconomic challenges that Janey faced upon graduating from Stanford, she had to contend with her parents' view of American society. Janey and I were married in a cathedral wedding at Old St. Mary's Church on the edge of San Francisco's Chinatown in July 1961. We move to Portland, Oregon, where I began graduate studies in physiology at the University of Oregon Medical School. Janey's parents counseled her against having a career and advised her to instead work as a laboratory technician to support me during my graduate studies and assume her natural feminine role. They thought that was the practical thing to do. That was also the prevalent attitude of American society. I convinced her to apply for a graduate fellowship at the University of Oregon Medical School. She was granted a fellowship by the Microbiology Department to conduct independent research in microbiology. It was not surprising that Janey's parents held very conservative views. Her father had been raised to be an obedient son in the Confucian tradition. Mary had been schooled in Shanghai and was unfamiliar with American mores. Both of her parents believed in educating their daughters, but also advocated for

American society's belief in the "natural role" of educated women as wife, mother, and housewife. Mary firmly told Janey she could not become a doctor because she would never find a husband. Yet, as you will read in Janey's letters in this book, she wanted a career in medicine. Her dilemma reached a crucial point when she arrived at a breakthrough moment for independent research at the time when Betty Friedan's book *The Feminine Mystique*, published in 1963, challenged the concept of women's natural role. Friedan claimed that there was more for educated women: they could be wives, mothers, and housewives and also have a career.

Janey proved that Betty Friedan was right. Over the next five decades, she was a curriculum developer and systems engineer at Bell Laboratories, one of the first two women and the only Asian American woman to receive the highest technical award at that company, and associate director of the Institute for Science, Technology, and Social Education at Rutgers University. She earned her EdD in psychology and education at Rutgers, did graduate studies and independent research in immunology at the University of Oregon Medical School, was a California State certified microbiologist, worked in the laboratory of a Nobel Prize winner as an undergraduate at Stanford, and received an A.B. in medical microbiology. She was also the wife of a neurophysiologist/public historian/ marketing consultant/Catholic deacon, mother of three sons, housewife, active in multiple community organizations, a skier and sailor, and chef and she served on the Environmental Commission of Franklin Township, New Jersey. Many of these facts were mentioned in her obituary following her death in May 2015. And yet, she was an enigmatic figure to family, friends, and even myself. She was like a multifaceted jewel, and some facets she didn't care to share with others. On the other hand, she could have said that about me. We both led very busy lives that intersected and intertwined. We knew, in general, what the other was doing but not many of the details. We didn't share details of our work with each other. On one occasion, I mentioned to her that I had received a consulting assignment with Bell Labs. She innocently asked, "What are you doing for them?" I hesitated and finally blurted out, "I can't tell you. It's client confidential."

My motives for writing this book are many, but uppermost, I wanted to discover how Janey accomplished all that she did and share lessons from her lifetime experiences with girls and women, encourage them to discover what they do best, and diligently pursue a career of their choice. To accomplish these goals I have used excerpts from Janey's 167 letters to me (about 700 handwritten pages), her Bell Laboratories personnel file, interviews with two of her Stanford roommates, and an oral history interview I conducted with her shortly after our 50th wedding anniversary in 2011 .

This book consists of four parts. Each part presents a different aspect of Janey's life. Part 1 is a synopsis of the 1960s era, when Janey wrote her letters during our 15-month long-distance courtship when we were students and separated by 560 miles from Stanford's campus in Palo Alto to the Eugene campus of the University of Oregon. The number of letters she wrote was extraordinary, and the cost of postage and telephone calls was equally extraordinary by today's standards. Part 2 contains excerpts from the letters sorted into 12 categories and presented chronologically within each topic. They illustrate specific moments and aspects of our relationship during our courtship as well as Janey's thoughts about her career. In each letter, Janey expressed all her thoughts about every subject that came to mind on that particular day—her wishes, desires, concerns, and thoughts about her future. They create a window into her mind that would be closed after our wedding and not opened again for five decades. The excerpts probably represent about one-quarter of the text from all the letters. Janey and I exchanged about the same number of letters. I spent my days at the University of Oregon conducting research in my advisor's laboratory when I wasn't studying. In the evening I would write a letter to Janey. I've kept all of her letters in two large file boxes that survived through eight household moves since 1961. Janey said she initially kept my letters but didn't remember what eventually happened to them. There are hints in her letters of what I wrote to her. I have provided an introduction to each topic to create a context for Janey's letters.

Part 3 is an effort to reveal and understand the internal and external forces that energized and motivated Janey to do what she did in her career and personal activities. She had a very complex personality and was very private at the same time. Soon after our wedding, she said, "It's very important to me to have some private time every day." I have used Michael Sloot's contemporary definition of the ancient Chinese yin and yang philosophy to examine her more dominant personality traits from a vantage point 60 years further along our journey. An incident when she challenged me and said, "Why are you lying?" opened my mind to truly understanding Janey's mindset and changed how I communicated with her from that moment forward. Janey's breakthrough moment in her career was when she overcame her doubts about being capable of doing independent research. Three mentors lifted her over her mental barrier when she was working as a laboratory assistant in the laboratory of a Nobel Prize winner.

In Part 4 Janey tells her life story in her own voice. It begins with a transcript of the oral history mentioned above, which we did together in the New York studio of StoryCorps. Janey was diagnosed with a terminal brain disease nine years earlier but at the time of the interview, she was mentally lucid and able to speak clearly. She was 73 years old. The interview was the "bookend" of her life story, complementing the letters she wrote in 1960 and 1961. Part 4 concludes with "Stanford

Memories," which Janey wrote on her page of the class of 1960's 50th class reunion book.

The gestation period for this book has been quite long. I suspect I've been subconsciously thinking about this book for six years since Janey's passing. However, the birthing process was quite brief. I began writing on a flight from New York to Anchorage on the way to Denali National Park. The first draft of the manuscript was completed five months later. I attribute the brevity of the writing process to the benefits of a change of scenery as well as writing amidst scholars laboring in the monastic silence of the Wertheim Study Room at the main branch of the New York Public Library.

Miller's Law of psychology says that the average person's short-term memory is capable of simultaneously remembering seven items, plus or minus two. Occasionally someone will ask, "What was it like to be married to Janey for 50 years?" It seemed that five decades passed by so quickly because we were so busy with our careers, volunteer activities, and raising a family. So my immediate response to the question is to mention one or two things that come to mind. Writing this book has given me the opportunity to reflect upon and better understand a lifetime spent with my soulmate.

Part 1

The 1960s: Paving the Way for a New Role for Women

As Janey Cheu graduated from Stanford University in 1960, the United States, along with much of the rest of the world, was about to enter a period of intense cultural and political upheaval that would be marked by a counterculture revolution in clothing, music, art, hallucinogenic drugs, and sexuality; the carnage of the War in Vietnam and violent student protests against it; and the assassinations of John F. Kennedy, Robert Kennedy, and Martin Luther King, Jr. Most importantly for Janey, a profound change in how women conceived of their roles in society and the home and their demands for equality was taking shape in the feminist movement. In what follows we trace the history of the 20th century retrospectively, beginning with the deceptively idyllic start of the presidency of John F. Kennedy and then going back to World War II and the Great Depression to set the stage for the arrival of baby boomers, American consumerism, and Betty Friedan's *The Feminine Mystique*. Like all of us, Janey Young was a product of her cultural heritage, her family, and the historical moment when she came of age—mixed with a determination to create her life as she imagined it regardless of social norms or family influence.

Camelot: The Kennedy Years

Don't let it be forgot
That once there was a spot
For one brief shining moment that was known
As Camelot
            —Alan Jay Lerner, "Camelot"

In an interview with *Life Magazine* following President John F. Kennedy's funeral on November 25, 1963, Jacqueline Kennedy said, "There will be great presidents again, but there will never be another Camelot." Her reference to the mythical realm of King Arthur and his Knights of the Roundtable gave the 1,036-day Kennedy presidency a special place in the history of American presidents. Jacqueline Kennedy's dubbing of the Kennedy era as "Camelot" reflected how the country saw the Kennedys as its royal family. The head of the family was young, handsome, a war hero, and intellectual, with a gentle sense of humor and ability to totally control the press corps and audiences with his presence. Jacqueline's sense of grace, the latest French fashions she wore, her flawless French that charmed European visitors and diplomats, and her eloquent poise certainly created the aura of a queen. The presence of two young children completed the image of a young royal family living in the White House. Jacqueline Kennedy's sense of the country's presidential history created a mythical memory of the Kennedy years that continues to the present day. By happenstance, the musical *Camelot*, with lyrics by Alan Lerner—a Harvard classmate of President Kennedy—and music by Frederick Lowe, made its Broadway debut in 1960, the year that Kennedy was elected. It quickly became a favorite of the American public, ran for 873 performances on Broadway, won multiple Tony Awards, and resulted in a 1967 movie version, foreign productions, and a revival in 2007, all of which helped sustain and continue Jacqueline Kennedy's vision of the American Camelot.

Americans have long been enthralled with English royalty. In the Declaration of Independence, Thomas Jefferson described the English king's abuse of the American colonies as the reason for declaring independence from England: "The history of the present King of Great Britain is a history of repeated injuries and usurpations, all having in direct object the establishment of an absolute Tyranny over these States." Despite more than three centuries of separation between the United States and Great Britain, the sister nations retain an emotional tie to one another. When President Biden and British Prime Minister Boris Johnson met for the first time, President Biden referred to "this 'special relationship' between Great Britain and the United States," a term said to have been coined by Winston Churchill in his first meeting with President Roosevelt during World War II. Many Americans have a continuing fascination with British royalty. An estimated 17.1 million viewers watched Oprah's 2021 interview of Meghan Markle and Prince Harry on CBS television, with a predominantly younger audience than for traditional prime-time specials. An article appeared in *Forbes* magazine with the headline "How Harry And Meghan Left Camelot For A More Quiet Life In America." It seems that the United States has now acquired its own royal couple with the potential to continue the Camelot saga.

John F. Kennedy was a charismatic leader who convinced Americans that they had a responsibility to help people in less wealthy nations and to serve their own country. When presidential candidate Kennedy spoke briefly to students gathered at the University of Michigan in an impromptu speech at 2:00 a.m. on October 14, 1960, he asked them if they were willing to volunteer to work overseas in developing countries to further world peace. He wasn't scheduled to speak at the university, but only intended to get a few hours of sleep before going on a whistle-stop train tour throughout Michigan later in the day. The students had been waiting for hours for his appearance. A microphone had been set up as if someone knew he would say something to the mass of students gathered in front of the student union building. The dean of women relaxed the 10:00 p.m. curfew for women students so they could be outside their dormitories and witness Kennedy's appearance on the campus. In what he described as his "longest short speech," which only lasted three minutes, he asked the assembled crowd, "How many of you who are going to be doctors are willing to spend your days in Ghana? Technicians or engineers, how many of you are willing to work in the Foreign Service and spend your lives traveling around the world? On your willingness to contribute part of your life to this country, I think will depend the answer whether a free society can compete."

Kennedy's questions to the students were the moment when he gave voice to the creation of the Peace Corps. It was a clarion call to the Michigan students to spend a few years of their lives serving their nation by serving people in underdeveloped countries and places they may not have even heard of. The response from the students was immediate and vigorous. Within a few days, several hundred had signed a pledge to volunteer. Two days before the election, a committee of Michigan students met with candidate Kennedy and presented him with a list of 800 students willing to volunteer for service in the Peace Corps. As word of the Michigan students' actions spread to other campuses, the Kennedy campaign began to receive pledges from hundreds of students across the nation.

In his inaugural speech, President Kennedy told the American people, "My fellow Americans: ask not what your country can do for you, ask what you can do for your country." Underlying that statement was a commitment by the new administration to create a Peace Corps, a task given to Kennedy's brother-in-law, Sargent Shriver. Shriver moved quickly to create a unique federal agency, independent of other government bureaucracies, providing paid, youthful volunteers trained to assist the local community wherever assigned, and open to all American applicants regardless of race or gender. In the 1960s, that was contrary to the norm of American employment practices. Newspaper job advertisements routinely listed jobs available for "men only." Other criteria, such as race, ethnicity, and religion, were among the well-known unwritten employment restrictions that job seekers had to consider when scanning the help wanted ads.

On August 30, 1961, only 19 months into the Kennedy administration, the first group of Peace Corps volunteers arrived at their foreign assignment in Accra, Ghana, including 50 teachers (21 women and 29 men). More than 240,000 volunteers have served in 142 countries since the formation of the Peace Corps six decades ago in 1961.

Kennedy's vision for better world relations, the Peace Corps, civil rights, and travel to the moon was cut short on November 22, 1963, when he was assassinated in Dallas, Texas.

Rebounds: The Great Depression to World War II

Newton's third law of physics—that for every action there is an equal and opposite reaction—can also be applied to the activities of humans. If two humans or groups of humans interact, each will exert a force on the other. The truth of this law of nature can be seen in relationships between husband and wife, economic competition between social groups, and warfare between nations. The 1950s were a rebound from two decades of economic and social adversity. First came the Great Depression of the 1930s.

In 1933, the worst year of the Depression, one-quarter of all workers, including agricultural workers, were unemployed. Those fortunate enough to still be employed saw their work hours reduced. Unemployment and a cutback in work hours greatly affected families because in most households only the husband worked. Women were more likely to lose their jobs during the Great Depression. In the 1930s 1.5 million women became unemployed, compared to 898,000

27

men. Increased mechanization reduced the need for semiskilled and unskilled workers, especially among men who were older, black, or both.

Millions of people lost their savings when more than one-third of all banks collapsed. Unregulated by the Federal Reserve Bank, banks stoked the nation's speculation in stocks by continuing to lend money to people to buy stocks on margin. They continued to lend money to businesses even as business inventories grew by 300% over the course of 1928 and 1929. When the economy turned down and depositors tried to withdraw their savings deposits, the majority of banks did not have enough cash reserves to meet the demand and closed their doors permanently.

The Great Depression ended in 1941 with the entry of the United States into World War II. Manufacturing companies changed to the production of war materiel; new production facilities were constructed for the production of weapons, ships, and airplanes; millions of men were drafted into the armed services; and women were recruited to fill the jobs vacated by the men gone to fight the wars in Europe, Africa, and Asia. On the home front, production of many consumer products ceased as raw materials were diverted to the production of military items. Automobile manufacturers stopped producing passenger cars and turned to manufacturing military vehicles. DuPont's introduction of women's nylon stockings in 1938 as a replacement for silk stockings was an immediate hit. During the war, nylon supplies were diverted to the production of parachutes, tires, and other critical military items. Nylon riots erupted during the war when women learned that stores had received a shipment of nylon stockings. Many consumer products were rationed, especially food items such as meat, butter, and sugar. Gasoline was in short supply for consumers and only people with a critical need for gasoline, such as doctors, were given gasoline rationing stamps. By the end of World War II there was considerable pent-up demand for consumer products not available during the war.

Wars are contradictory. Wars kill and traumatize combatants and civilians and destroy the structure of ordinary life. When the United States entered World War II, the Manhattan Project was initiated to build a functional atomic bomb before Hitler's regime could reach the same goal. The team of American scientists and military experts succeeded in detonating the first atomic bomb in New Mexico in July 1945. As the world knows, the two atomic bombs used against Japan decimated the cities of Hiroshima and Nagasaki, killed an estimated 100,000 people, and ended the war with Japan.

Throughout the history of warfare, more combatants died from infection than from battlefield wounds. During the Civil War, uncontrolled infections killed as many as two-thirds of the soldiers who died. Lost in the dusty pages of history is an American–British project greater and more important than the Manhattan Project that saved the lives of possibly a million or more American GIs, sailors, and airmen in World War II. The Penicillin Project grew out of the discovery of penicillin and its transformation into the first medication capable of killing infectious bacteria. In 1928, Scottish biologist Alexander Fleming discovered that the penicillin mold was capable of killing bacteria but he was only able to extract minute amounts of the antibacterial component from the mold. Samples of penicillin tested in a few patients demonstrated its ability to stop infections as no other medicines were capable of doing. Other scientists carried on Fleming's work to find a way to mass produce the critical penicillin element, an effort made even more urgent by the start of World War II in 1939. The importance of finding a way to make penicillin into a readily available medicine was imprinted on the minds of Allied military leaders expecting a high casualty rate among the 156,000 Allied troops landing on the beaches of Normandy against stiff German defenses on D-Day, June 6, 1944. In 1942, the U.S. Department of Defense created a poster urging a maximum effort to construct facilities to product penicillin. The headline read, "A Race Against Death!" The text said, "The Faster this building is completed, the quicker our wounded men get Penicillin—The New Life-Saving Drug. Give this job EVERYTHING You've got!"

The all-out effort to develop a practical penicillin medicine paid off. Hundreds of thousands of American servicemen did not die from incurable infectious wounds and diseases in World War II. They came home to take advantage of going to college on the GI Bill and entering fields not available to them before the war. They married the girlfriends who waited for their return, and had the children that created the baby boomer generation. The prosperity of the 1950s and 1960s was the result of so many healthy servicemen returning from war to reenter civilian life and create a higher standard of living than was possible before 1941.

A New Role for Women?

Whether we talk of Africa, Islam or Asia, women never had it so good as you [American] women do.
—Adlai E. Stevenson, Smith College
Commencement speech, 1955

During World War II, the drafting of thousands of American men for military duty created an employment vacuum in offices and factories across the United States. During the early years of the war, demand for war materials led to the construction of new manufacturing plants such as new shipyards on the East and West coasts. Women—all women, regardless of age or race—were recruited to work in the plants. For many women, especially middle-class women, this was the first time they worked outside their home and earned a wage. The famous Westinghouse poster of Rosie the Riveter appeared in 1943 and highlighted the role of women in the war effort. They did civilian jobs previously only available to men, from building every kind of military equipment, including tanks, ships, and airplanes, to flying the planes from the factories to airfields for pickup by military pilots.

Unlike World War I, when only two million men were sent overseas in 1916 as members of the American Expeditionary Force, there were more than 8 million U.S. military personnel overseas at the end of World War II, and virtually all were men. They were discharged as quickly as possible at the end of 1946. Returning servicemen expected that men and women would resume the gender roles in society that existed prior to the war. Betty Friedan defined the role of women as the "feminine mystique" in her 1963 book of the same name that shook the foundations of American culture. The feminine mystique was the assumption that American women should be fulfilled by their expected roles as housewives and mothers, and nothing more. Men were supposed to be good providers for their families and married women were to support their husbands so they could earn a good living. The husband was the head of the family and the wife was responsible for managing the household and raising the children.

The relationship between men and women was established soon after humans (homo sapiens) appeared on earth some 70,000 years ago, when clusters of people gathered for survival, according to historian Yuval Noah Harari in his very readable 2015 book *Sapiens*. The men were hunters and the women gathered vegetables and fished while tending to the children. The men were the leaders of their families and the women were the subordinate followers. The dominant relationship of men over women in Western culture was recorded 2,000 years ago in the *Letter to the Ephesians* of the New Testament of the Bible, which reads:

5:22 Wives, be subject to your husbands, as to the Lord.
5:23 For the husband is the head of the wife, as Christ also is the head of the church, He himself being the Savior of the body,
5:24 But as the church is subject to Christ, so also the wives ought to be to their Husbands in everything.

For more than 2,000 years, Christian churches have accepted the New Testament of the Bible as authoritative scripture, as the teachings of Jesus Christ. The belief that men were superior to women expressed in Ephesians was not a new concept. It was a long-existing belief among many cultures of the ancient world and continues to be cited in the 21st century by those who reject the idea of equality between women and men.

When Adlai Stevenson spoke to the 1955 graduating class of Smith College, a private women's institution, his commencement speech was based on the assumption that a "natural relationship" existed between men and women, as stated in *Ephesians*. He told the young women,

> You may be hitched to one of these creatures we call "Western man" and I think part of your job is to keep him Western, to keep him truly purposeful, to keep him whole. ...This assignment for you, as wives and mothers, has great advantages. In the first place, it is home—you can do it in the living-room with a baby in your lap or in the kitchen with a can opener in your hand. If you're really clever, maybe you can even practice your saving arts on that unsuspecting man while he's watching television!

The Age of Consumerism

Stevenson was voicing what American society believed: that the prosperity of the postwar years had created a golden age for housewives. A pent-up desire for consumer products not available during the war, savings accumulated when there was nothing to buy, the flight of whites to the suburbs into all-white Levittown communities built for the returning veterans and their families, labor-saving household products with advanced technology, and the power of a new advertising medium—television—all of these combined to establish an era of consumerism that focused on reducing the drudgery of housekeeping and giving the middle-class suburban American housewife more free time to pursue volunteer activities that strengthened the foundations of Western culture, but not necessarily work or a career.

In the years before World War II, housewives used a manual carpet sweeper or broom and dustpan to keep the carpets and floors clean. They washed the family laundry using an electric washing machine comprised of a large tub with an oscillating paddle with a gear handle that controlled the force and speed of the paddle. The machine was connected to the separate hot and cold water faucets. The housewife controlled the temperature of the water and how much water came into the tub for each cycle of washing and multiple rinses, and pumped the water out after each cycle. When the laundry was clean she fed each item of clothing into a wringer attached to the tub, which forced most of the water out of the clothes. Then she hung each item on outdoor clotheslines using wooden clothespins. The weekly family washing—perhaps done several times a week depending on the size of the family—was laborious, tiring, and time consuming. Preparing and cooking family meals was equally demanding. Iceboxes were used to keep food and milk cold. Blocks of ice were routinely delivered by the iceman and bottles of pasteurized milk were left at the front door by the milkman. When the kitchen became hot during the summer, electric fans circulated the warm air. After a meal, dishes, utensils, and pots and pans were hand washed. When the sun went down, households with electricity were lit by electric light bulbs that emitted a yellowish light and were half as bright as a 1960s light bulb. Sometimes they spontaneously exploded.

The diversion of U.S. manufacturing to produce war-related items created a pent-up demand for consumer products after the war at a time when the United States was the only major source of manufactured products in the world due to the massive destruction of factories and infrastructure in Europe during the war. By 1949,

American companies had sold millions of automobiles and household products, including refrigerators and stoves. In the 1950s and 1960s, technologies developed during the war were being used to develop new electric consumer products designed for middle-class suburban homes that reduced the labor and time to perform household chores. These new homes had sufficient space and electrical power for these products, which was not the case with older urban homes. A two-page 1960 Hotpoint advertisement for its All-Electric Kitchen represented the leading edge of kitchen technology designed for housewives. It promised, "Your dream kitchen is almost a reality. We mean the Hotpoint Electric Kitchen you and Jim have been saving War Bonds for. And it will be priced within easy reach of folks whose income is modest." The Hotpoint kitchen offered the housewife an electric stove with a timer-controlled broiler oven, an electric garbage disposal, an automatic dishwasher, and an electric refrigerator with ice-making and frozen food storage. While few young families could afford to purchase all these appliances at one time, it was possible to begin with one appliance, perhaps a refrigerator or stove, and buy others as their savings allowed.

Hotpoint's advertising pitch to housewives was based on a revolutionary development in consumer financing that began when Bank of America introduced its BankAmericard in 1958. Prior to 1958, consumer products were purchased C.O.D. (cash on delivery). The only way to purchase a product or service was to wait until you had saved enough money. U.S. Government war bonds and savings bonds competed with banks for people's savings. The BankAmericard offered consumers two very important features. First, it could be used wherever it was accepted by a merchant, including stores and restaurants. More importantly, the balance did not have to be paid when the bill arrived from Bank of America. Instead, the balance could be reduced each month until it was paid off. Of course, Bank of America charged interest on the unpaid balance, which generated a profit for the bank. By 1960, as many as 1 million BankAmericards had been issued to consumers. Six years later, more than 61,000 merchants across the nation accepted the card for purchases.

A podcast by John Macce and Sam Stentz titled *American Consumerism in the 1950's* describes how prosperous the United States was at that time: "In the 1950's the overall economy grew by 37%. By the end of the decade the median American family had 30% more purchasing power than at the beginning. Unemployment during the decade dropped to as low as 4.5%. In the 50's the boosted economy caused people to want to spend, and spend they did." The difference between the American economies of the 1950s and 1960s and that of the 1930s and 1940s is quite remarkable.

In 1960, 78% of American households had a telephone and 88% had a television set. A third and major element in the creation of the era of consumerism in the 1950s and 1960s was the role of television in making consumers aware of the vast array of new products available in the marketplace. Television was the game changer in motivating consumers to buy new products seen in television commercials. There is an adage in the advertising industry that "You can't sell a refrigerator to an Eskimo." You may not be able to sell a refrigerator to an Inuit hunter living in the frigid northern reaches of Alaska, but he might be tempted to buy a more reliable and improved snowmobile seen on television at the village community center. Between 1950 and 1960, total advertising expenditures doubled from $6 billion to $12 billion and their share of the GDP increased from 1.9% to 2.3%. Among the top 1960 consumer product advertisers, the percent of advertising dollars spent on television ranged from 24% by General Motors, which favored advertising in magazines, to 93% by Proctor and Gamble, the country's second largest advertiser. The appeal of television to advertisers is its ability to combine entertainment with a sales pitch. In 1960, nearly half of the American population was under 25 and active visual media such as television and movies were particularly attractive to this group.

Making Up for Lost Time: Four Million Babies a Year!

The entry of the United States into War World II changed forever the relationship between young women and men recently graduated from high school or 18 years and older. They were predominately from working-class families and had not traveled far from where they were born and grew up. Prior to the war, they expected to do what their parents had done: get married and assume their expected gender roles in society. During the war, suddenly millions of young men were uprooted from civilian life, cast into a regimented life with strangers from all parts of the country, and found themselves far from their high school sweethearts. The greatest concern of World War II servicemen, other than being killed or wounded in battle, was whether the girl left behind would be waiting for them when they got home again. The anticipated regular mail call when incoming mail was distributed to the eagerly waiting soldiers, sailors, or airmen was always clouded with the fear that the next letter from home would be a "Dear John" letter from the girl back home saying she had met another man.

When the war finally ended on September 2, 1945, the men returned to their hometowns and their girlfriends, anxious to make up for the lost war years. This generation of Americans had a remarkably high marriage rate: 96% of the women and 94% of the men married. They had more children, more quickly, than the generations before them. In 1935 at the depth of the Great Depression, the U.S. birthrate was 19 live births per 1,000 people. Beginning in 1945, the birth rate started to climb and remained above 25 per 1,000 through the 1950s. From 1954 through 1964, more than 4 million babies were born each year. The dramatic increase in the birth rate in the postwar years can be seen in these U.S. Census numbers:

Year	Live Births (millions)	Birthrate per 1,000
1930	2.62	21.3
1935	2.38	18.7
1945	2.86	20.4
1950	3.63	24.1
1955	4.10	25.0
1960	4.26	23.7

The United States was youthful in the 1960s: one-half of the population was 29 years or younger.[1] Like their parents, many of this generation married early. First-time brides were 20 years old and their husbands were three years older. However, more women high school graduates (38%) were attending college than before, along with 54% of men. In 1960, American colleges and universities awarded 392,440 bachelor's degrees. Two-thirds were received by men and one-third by women. That same year, 25,353 first professional degrees were awarded in chiropracty, dentistry, law, medicine, optometry, osteopathic medicine, pharmacy, podiatry, theology, and veterinary medicine.[2] Women earned 3% of 1,112 doctorate degrees but only 676 of first professional degrees, including doctor of medicine degrees.[3]

For most women, attending or graduating from college did not lead to further education and a career. Nearly half of Americans disapproved of a married woman earning money if her husband could support her. Thus a college degree did not change the dictate of the feminine mystique that being a wife and mother was enough for women.

1 Frank Hobbs and Nicole Stoops, *Demographic Trends in the 20th Century* (Washington, D.C.: U.S. Census Bureau, 2002), p. 57, https://www.census.gov/prod/2002pubs/censr-4.pdf.
2 "U.S. Census Decennial Census 1960," https://www.census.gov/programs-surveys/decennial-census/decade/decennial-publications.1960.html
3 "U.S. Census of Population: 1960 Education Attained," https://www2.census.gov/library/publications/decennial/1960/population-volume-2/41927945v2p5a-5cch2.pdf

"A Finishing School Disguised as a College"

Professor: After graduation you can have a marriage and a career.
Student: Why would I do that?
—Mona Lisa Smile

The 2003 movie *Mona Lisa Smile* takes place in the fall of 1953 at Wellesley College, an elite women's college established in Wellesley, Massachusetts, in 1870. A recent graduate of a California university, graduate student Katherine Watson (played by Julia Roberts) has been hired to teach a class in art history. She brings with her ideas about woman's identity and their role in society that challenge established beliefs at Wellesley. Although the movie is fictional, it portrays what most Americans in the 1950s and 1960s felt about the role of women, regardless of their level of education. In the manners classroom in the film Miss Abbey (Marcia Gay Harden) is giving a required class on etiquette and manners to the Wellesley students and she reprimands a student who jokes about marriage, telling her, "A few years from now, your sole responsibility will be taking care of your husband and children." In the following exchange in Katherine Watson's office, student Joan Brandyn (Julia Stiles) is complaining about receiving a C on a paper. She sees her personal file on Watson's desk.

Joan: Is that my file on your desk? What does it say?
Watson: Your major is pre-law. What law school are you going for?
Joan: I really hadn't thought about that. After graduation I plan on getting married.
Watson: And then?
Joan: And then I'll be married.
Watson: You can do both. Just for fun, if you could go to any law school in the country, which would it be?
Joan: Yale. They keep five slots open for women and unofficially one for a Wellesley girl.
Watson: But you really haven't thought about it?
Joan: No.

Later, in a lecture hall, Professor Watson hands out a test. As she walks by Joan, she casually drops a Yale Law School application on Joan's desk. Joan doesn't react, but Watson has made an impression on her. In a later scene, Joan is talking with her engaged friend Betty (Kirsten Durst):

Joan: You have everything you ever dreamed of. I have a secret. I got accepted early to Yale Law School.
Betty: Why? You don't want to be a lawyer.
Joan: Maybe I do. I applied on a lark. Never thought we'd get in.
Betty: We?
Joan: Miss Watson. She practically filled out my application for me.
Betty: Why? You don't want to be a lawyer.
Joan: First of all, there's no ring on this finger. Second, I can do both. I can.
Betty: How does Tony [Joan's boyfriend] feel about this?
Joan: No one knows.
Betty: You're this close to getting everything you wanted and you're this close to losing it.

When the college imposes restrictions on Katherine Watson as a condition of further employment, she tells her class, "I give up. You are the smartest women in the country. I didn't realize that by demanding excellence I'd be challenging—what did it say in that school newspaper editorial—'the roles you were born to fill?' Is that right? Roles you were born to fill?" She later chides President Carr in a similar vein:

Watson: These girls, are you proud, President Carr?
Carr: Yes, I am.
Watson: I guess you should be. Half are married and the other half give it a month or so. That's what they're doing. Biding their time until someone proposes.

Finally, Katherine Watson bursts into an Italian class taught by Professor Bill Dunbar (Dominic West) and declares, "To hell with Wellesley. I'm done. It's a perfect ruse. A finishing school disguised as a college. I thought I was headed to a place to turn out tomorrow's leaders, not their wives."

Stanford University: A 1960s Elite Women's Finishing School

The Stanford University class of 1960 included 1,214 students: 758 men (62%) and 456 women (38%). Racially, 99% of the students were white. The remaining 1% of the class included five Asian Americans and one black student. Women of the class of 1960 received the following letter about their attire prior to their arrival on campus in September 1956. (Men in the same class did not receive a letter telling them how to dress.) The letter tells the women students that they are expected to conform to Stanford's code of appearance for women students:

Suggestions For Clothes
Appropriate For Stanford

First of all, let me remind you that Stanford is really in the country and that there is a pleasant informality on the campus. We are suggesting to you a general wardrobe which the average girl at Stanford needs.

In your classes, at movies in Palo Alto, at jolly-ups and informal dances, at football games, etc. you will need the following:

Skirts, blouses, and sweaters, wool sport dresses, and cottons or other cool dresses. (Sometimes we have very warm weather for several weeks in early fall; sometimes the cool weather beings early.) Sport coat and hat.

Low-heeled, comfortable shoes (essential for the walking necessary at Stanford. It is recommended that you bring a pair with you in your suitcase as a great deal of walking is necessary the first few days, and your trunk might be delayed.) High heels are reserved for dress occasions.

For teas, shopping or dances in San Francisco, faculty dinners, and Chapel:

A tailored suit and one or two silk dresses of street length. Dress coat, hat, gloves, and shoes.

For more dressy campus dances:

A formal and a coat or evening wrap. A dress suit and a long dinner dress might be useful, but they are not necessary.

A warm bathrobe is really necessary, for our evenings are cool.

A raincoat and boots are needed for the winter weather.

After you have arrived on campus, you may consult your sponsor concerning what you should wear on specific occasions. She will be glad to tell you anything further you might wish to know.

On arrival at campus, every student received a copy of the class Frosh Book, a tradition that began in 1945 with a class half as large as the class of 1960. It read:

Members of the Freshman Class of 1945

This book is an experiment. It contains the names, pictures, and home towns of the residents of Roble and Encina Halls … most of them in the Class of '45 with a few men of the class of '44 scattered throughout. We hope that it will help you know your freshmen and be able to associate their names with their faces.

By 1956, the *Frosh Book* had morphed into a *Dating Book*. The cover featured a cartoon of three freshman men dressed as Indian braves looking for their dream freshman woman. (*Freshman*, now often replaced by the gender-neutral *first-year student*, then referred to both male and female students.) The editors, Gary Willcuts and Ken Rose, wrote, "The Froshbook is needed by those who are getting blind dates with the prettier than ever freshman girls, and by clubs and fraternities who will soon be entering into their rushing programs." The last Froshbook was published in 1995, for the entering class of 1999. By this time, the dorms were co-ed. Surprisingly, my house in Wilbur Hall, Madera, no longer existed as a dorm. Dorms began to be co-ed in 1966.

Prior to arriving on campus, all entering women of the class of 1960 received by mail a 19-page, 8½ x 11-inch handbook with a cartoon on the cover depicting a Stanford woman student as an Indian squaw. Its title was "Social Standards, made by and for Women Students of Stanford University." It included 139 rules, regulations, and definitions to establish boundaries of acceptable social behavior for Stanford women living in university dormitories or off campus. Crossing a boundary without permission resulted in one or more penalties, which could be as extreme as "removal from the University." The handbook described the purpose of the regulations in these words:

> In accepting the privilege of being a Stanford woman, you are also accepting the Responsibility of meeting the highest standards of conduct and good taste in your actions at all times.... The main purpose of our social regulations system is to help develop social maturity, which means individual

and group responsibility. Therefore, one of the essential elements of the system, which insures its liberal nature, is the freedom of decision. Yet, another equally important basis of the system is its assumption that individual decisions will be accompanied by careful consideration of the standards maintained by the group. In this way, freedom of decision will not jeopardize the rights and freedoms of others, since each student at Stanford is not only an individual but also a part of a larger living group, the campus community, and society... The enforcement of the social regulations is through the demerit system.

There was no handbook of "Social Standards for Freshman Men." If the men had been subjected to the same social and dormitory regulations as the women, their number would have declined rapidly.

In September 1955, freshman men of the class of 1959 resided in a newly constructed residential complex, Wilbur Hall, consisting of eight separate houses with a total capacity of 700 men. Each house had a residential assistant (RA) who supervised residents' behavior. At Madera House, one of the eight Wilbur Hall houses, the RA was a varsity football player and frequently away when the football team traveled. I was a member of the class of 1959 men at Madera House. When the RA was off to a game, we were unsupervised from Friday to Sunday and we pretty much did whatever we wanted to do as long as another RA or the house master didn't become aware of what we were up to.

For some reason, my floor tended to be antisocial. One Saturday evening, a dance was being held on campus—not at Wilbur Hall—and nicely dressed first-year couples (women attired in accordance with the Stanford Social Regulations) were seen walking by Madera. Several men on the floor formed a team and built a very large slingshot and used it to propel water balloons at passing couples. Fortunately, their aim was bad. On another occasion, several men returned to campus intoxicated. One of them was quite short and nicknamed Shorty. Two of the other drunk men put Shorty into a large laundry dryer in the basement, added some coins, and everyone laughed as Shorty spun around and around. The RA may have heard about the incident because it was never repeated. Telephone calls from the campus to anywhere other than the local town of Palo Alto were expensive long-distance calls. One member of our floor devised a gadget that could be inserted into the end of the telephone receiver and bypass the coin circuitry, allowing for free phone calls. Everyone on the floor had one. The RA never said not to use it. He may very well have used it too.

In his 2003 review of *Mona Lisa Smile* in the *Observer*, Andrew Sarris points out that the screenplay was inspired by a magazine article by Hillary Rodham Clinton about her years at Wellesley in the 1960s and was reset by the screenwriters in "the Eisenhower era—a time when women were still being exhorted to become happy housewives and forget that they'd capably (and profitably) performed men's jobs during World War II....Wellesley's current administration cooperated fully with the producers, and why not? There is no contemporary institutional disgrace in admitting the fact that a half-century ago, according to [screenwriter Lawrence] Konner, 'they were doing French literature in the morning, and how to serve tea to your husband's boss in the afternoon.'"

In the 1960s, on the West Coast across the continent from Wellesley, was an actual elite private university, Stanford, that did its best to ensure that its women students conformed to the socially defined role for young American women who, the administration believed, would inherit the feminine mystique.

Part 2

Janey's Love Letters

1. Introduction

Dickinson was capitalizing upon a technique women have always known and used, for survival, using the imagination as a space in which to create some life other than their external situation.
—Suzanne Juhasz, *The Undiscovered Continent*

Growing up Asian American in California

Most of San Francisco's Chinese American youth were trapped in the confines of Chinatown by racially motivated restrictive property covenants, inadequate English language skills, and large-scale illegal immigration from China since the passage of the Chinese Exclusion Act of 1882. This was not Janey's case. Her childhood was shaped by three cultures: Chinese, American, and Chinese American. During World War II she lived in Whittier, California, 20 miles southeast of Los Angeles, with her parents and grandparents. The Whittier experience provided her—perhaps "equipped" is a better word—with positive aspects of the American and Chinese cultures. At home, speaking Cantonese with her parents and grandparents provided her with both fluency and subtle lessons in Chinese culture, for language is culture. In elementary school, her classmates were white, the teachers were white, and she learned to speak English fluently without a trace of the Chinese accent that was so common with Chinese youth who grew up in San Francisco's Chinatown. At the time, Whittier was home to many retired missionaries, including some who had served in China, and they were supportive and nurturing of this "cute Chinese family" in Whittier. Each missionary wanted Janey, and later her sister, to attend the Sunday school of their denomination, as Janey mentions in her letters.

Although she did not live in Chinatown for very long, her residence there occurred during her formative preteen years and made her very aware of the social and economic constraints that racism placed on Chinatown's residents. Moreover, the livelihood of her father and the extended family through their soy sauce factory depended on a Chinatown economy based on tourism.

The family's move to the Richmond district of San Francisco allowed Janey to attend the diversified local public high school where pop singer Johnny Mathis was a few years ahead of her. Her high school experience gave her opportunities to develop social and academic skills and participate in extracurricular activities such as the Model United Nations that would play a role in her social and academic future at Stanford.

My mother, Nellie Ruth Ohn, was the daughter of her father's second wife, who he married in China after his first wife gave birth to a daughter rather than the son. My mother's father came to the United States possibly sometime in the 1880s to replace his cousin as the superintendent of the Ferry Morse Company seed farm, near Gilroy, California, the largest commercial U.S. seed producer at the time. Prior to working for Ferry Morse, the cousin worked at the Leland Stanford farm, which became the campus of Stanford University. During the growing season, the farm could employ as many as 200 Chinese laborers. Seeds were collected for some crops manually by tying paper bags over the seeds and shaking the mature seeds into the bags.

My mother was born in San Francisco and lived on the Ferry Morse farm as a child. She attended school in Gilroy and graduated from Gilroy High School as the class valedictorian. Her friends and classmates were white and she did not speak Chinese except for a few phrases with her mother. Her father was Westernized, was fluent in Chinese and English, and joined the Chinese Methodist Church in San Francisco's Chinatown. After her parents died during her teenage years, my mother was adopted by Dr. and Mrs. Elmer Chesbro of Gilroy, who were long-time friends of her father. The Chesbros were a prominent medical family in Gilroy and community leaders. They made it possible for my mother to enroll in the nursing program at San Francisco's Children's Hospital at a time when Asian American women were not accepted in the nursing programs at private hospitals. She graduated in 1928, married my father in 1929 after he graduated from Stanford Medical School, and worked as a nurse as he attempted to establish a medical practice in Chinatown during the Depression.

My father, Henry Docfoo Cheu, was born in China in the rural village of Nam Moon in the Pearl River delta and was sent to the United States alone at age 14 to fulfill his parents' goal for him to become a doctor, with the assumption that he would return to China to practice medicine and support the family. By virtue of his birth in China, my father was subject to the Chinese Exclusion Act of 1882. He migrated to the United States illegally using a "paper son" scheme, claiming to be the son of a Chinese immigrant who was a U.S. citizen. When my parents married, the Cable Act of 1922 automatically stripped my mother of her American birthright for marrying "an alien ineligible for American citizenship." She became a person without a country.

My parents were forced to live in segregated Chinatown so that my father could practice medicine. My mother was a social outcast there since she didn't speak Chinese and my parents seldom if ever attended Chinatown social affairs as a couple. Her friends were her acquaintances

47

from Gilroy and nursing school. She was adamant that I would not develop the Chinglish accent common to the youth of Chinatown. As we walked, she would drill me on spelling and speech. One of the first words I learned to spell and pronounce was "otolaryngology." My mother was an education activist. In 1948 she became the first Asian American PTA president outside of Chinatown, an achievement resented and resisted by some of the white parents at Francisco Junior High School and residents near the school in North Beach.

Like Janey, I did not attend Galileo High School, which many if not most of Chinatown's teenagers attended. I attended Lowell High, the public school system's academic high school, where admission was based on academic record and passing the entrance examination. I entered Stanford as a freshman in September 1955 and graduated with the class of 1959.

How Janey and I Met

"I Could Write a Book"

If they asked me, I could write a book
About the way you walk and whisper and look
I could write a preface on how we met
So the world would not forget

And the simple secret of the plot
Is just to tell them that I love you, a lot

Then the world discovers as my book ends
How to make two lovers of friends
—From the musical *Pal Joey*, by Richard Rodgers and Lorenz Hart

My mother was bedridden during my high school years and I cared for her after school each day. On the weekends, I did the family laundry and cleaned the three-story home that had been built to Dad's design. My mother died during the fall quarter of my freshman year at

Stanford. I spent my sophomore year at the University of California, Berkeley, commuting daily from home in San Francisco and returning home to care for my father and manage the household. The added chore while I was at UC was cooking dinner during the week. Dad arrived home from his office in Chinatown at precisely 6:00 p.m. and expected dinner to be ready. I could tell he had arrived when I heard the electric garage door opening. The commute to Berkeley and the need to have dinner ready when Dad came home meant that I had virtually no social life during my sophomore year because I was also my father's companion on the weekends after my mother's death.

I attended only one social event at UC, when a few Stanford Chinese students came to UC to attend a dance. Of course I was very interested to meet the very small contingent of Chinese American students at Stanford that travelled from Palo Alto, across San Francisco Bay, to Berkeley. I met Janey at the dance and thought she was rather distant, perhaps reflecting a bias among Stanford men, who regarded Stanford women as "really smart but not great socially." When I returned to Stanford for my junior year, Janey and I met again and chatted at the Chinese Students Club meetings, but we dated only occasionally during my final two years at Stanford. This all changed on New Year's Eve 1959, after I had graduated and was at the University of Oregon studying for a master's degree in biology.

What Is Love?

It may come as a shock to some prospective brides and bridegrooms that love is a four-stage process and love can fail at any of the stages. I have come to this conclusion based on personal experiences with marriage and as a Catholic deacon. Janey and I passed through all four stages of love in our 54-year marriage before she died. As an ordained deacon, I have worked with parishioners in all aspects of marriage: marriage preparation, conducting marriage ceremonies, marriage counseling, and annulment. In my view, based on my experience as a deacon involved in marital matters and my 54 years of marriage, the traditional stages of love are:

1. *Expression*: emotional, physical, and conversational
2. *Acceptance*: engagement
3. *Commitment:* marriage (public vows)
4. *Trust*: living the vow

The expression of love between two people usually follows a period of friendship when both people develop an increasing sense of affection for the other that is expressed emotionally and physically and accompanied by a desire to be with each other. It is not the result of intellectual analysis but simply the unexplainable chemistry between two people that builds to an emotional summit. Sometimes referred to as a "crush" or "puppy love," it can disappear as quickly as it appears. However, expressions of love shouldn't be too quickly dismissed. It was Sigmund Freud who noted the "proverbial durability of first loves." Acceptance of love is expressed through a public ritual such as engagement or "pinning" of a young woman by her fraternity boyfriend, in which the girl wears the fraternity's pin as a public display of their relationship. Members of Stanford's all-male Eating Clubs pinned girls in the 1950s and 1960s. Commitment of love between two people is also a public ritual—the wedding in which the bride and groom profess a vow of commitment. For Catholics and Protestants the vow focuses on the commitment to each other "for better or worse." In secular weddings, where a "minister" can be ordained online for as little as $30 to perform the marriage ceremony, the couple may design their own vows. Regardless of how the couple is married, the true test of love is in the fourth stage. Trust is determined by whether both parties live a life committed to their vow, which is revealed over time.

Four out of every ten American first marriages do not reach the fourth stage of love and end in divorce. Janey's letters reveal how we moved through the first three stages of love. Her oral history in part 4 of this book describes how we experienced the fourth stage of love.

What Janey's Letters Reveal

From January 1960 to March 1961, Janey and I were 560 miles apart. She was a senior at Stanford and I was working on my master's at the University of Oregon. The letters reflect Janey's side of our conversations. Each of her letters was all encompassing: she wrote about anything and everything on her mind that particular day.

I have selected excerpts from the letters that focus on our developing relationship, our relationship with our parents, and the critical issue of Catholicism that could have prevented our marriage. Underlying these concerns was the reality that Chinese Americans were not fully accepted as Americans in the era of these letters. At two separate New Jersey volunteer fire departments, my application for membership was challenged because I was an Asian American, even though I had served as an officer in another volunteer fire department. The first time I attended a monthly meeting of the Red Bank, New Jersey, fire department, someone shouted, "Who let the chink in?" Two years later, I was elected captain of an engine company in that department. A former captain of the company told me, "You're the best captain we've ever had." I persisted because I remembered Harry Truman saying, "If you can't stand the heat, get out of the kitchen."

The excerpts from Janey's letters are organized by categories and arranged chronologically within each category to reveal Janey's evolving views on topics integral to us and our individual development as we planned a future life together. There are two persistent themes in Janey's letters: a desire for a career, and that love is forever. About her desire for a career she wrote, "I don't want to be a lab tech for the rest of my life."

As for love, whenever we passed a lake or pond and saw two ducks swimming together, she would say, "See those two ducks? They're together for life. Don't you forget that!"

2. The Date That Changed Our Lives

I was so pleased to receive Janey's invitation to attend her cousin's birthday party on New Year's Eve 1959, an annual event held at Kan's Restaurant in San Francisco's Chinatown. I had never had a meal there. My father thought it was a tourist trap, when equally good Chinese food was available at many less expensive restaurants in Chinatown. Janey's father and his brother-in-law were partners in Johnny Kan's restaurant.

Johnny Kan had a natural instinct for identifying new ways to satisfy people's hunger within the 16 blocks of Chinatown. He started Fong Fong's bakery and ice cream parlor in 1935 and transformed it into "the" place for American-born Chinese teenagers and college students. He introduced Chinese ice cream flavors like lychee to satisfy tourists. In 1939 he started the Chinese Kitchen on the western perimeter of Chinatown, the first Chinese takeout restaurant in the San Francisco Bay Area. In 1953 he established his signature restaurant, Johnny Kan's, on Chinatown's main thoroughfare, Grant Avenue, based on the concept of presenting authentic Cantonese cuisine in an elegant venue. This was not the first attempt at Chinese haute cuisine in Chinatown but it was the first truly successful venture. In the prosperity of the postwar decades, when tourists were no longer afraid to venture into Chinatown, he catered to a growing interest in authentic Chinese food, particularly among veterans who had served in Asia during World War II. It was the first successful postwar Chinatown restaurant offering an authentic, haute cuisine Cantonese dining experience. Kan's received the *Holiday Magazine* Award for Fine Dining for 14 consecutive years and was listed in the Top Ten Restaurants of San Francisco.

Johnny Kan was the culinary impresario of Chinatown in the postwar decades. His outsized personality attracted the attention of San Francisco columnist Herb Caen. The restaurant's success was due in no small part to the frequent mention of Kan's in Herb Caen's immensely popular daily gossip column in the *San Francisco Chronicle*. The column frequently commented about Hollywood celebrities seen there, including Danny Kaye, who was a master chef in addition to his theatrical talents. He became a good friend of Johnny Kan, who occasionally—unknown to the customers—allowed Danny to cook a dish on a customer's order. He would secretively peer out of the kitchen into the dining area, hoping to see if the customers enjoyed his cooking.

When the birthday party ended, the night was still young. I suggested to Janey that we walk down to the Embarcadero and take a water taxi tour around San Francisco Bay. It seemed like a fun idea and it appealed to her sense of adventure, so she agreed. We arrived at the Embarcadero only to discover that the water taxis were on strike. The only alternative was a stroll along the waterfront. As we were walking, we saw a single lit building and I convinced Janey that we should go in and find out if there was an alternative to hiring a water taxi. A very friendly man sitting at a desk greeted us. When he heard what we wanted to do he said, "Wait a minute, kids." He turned and said into a microphone, "I'm going out for a while on the boat." It turned out that he was the Bay pilot on duty, waiting for any ship requiring a pilot to bring it into San Francisco Harbor, a very unlikely event on New Year's Eve. He led us to the harbor pilot's tugboat and the three of us climbed on board. To our stunned amazement, he took us on a guided tour of San Francisco Bay. A few days later, I brought a box of San Francisco's favorite candies, See's Candy, to the office for him and Janey sent him a gift.

Janey and I were Stanford students at the same time for two years before I graduated in June 1959. We saw each other at the monthly Chinese Students Club meetings and passed by each other on campus, but only had one date in those two years. After our New Year's Eve date, we became seriously interested in each other. Janey remembered this date in three letters.

January 26, 1960

Yes, your thank you was in order—I did send Mr. Lock the
note of deep gratitude complete with a picture of our alma
mater and all. I can't help but wonder if he ever received
it, though, as you can guess, I don't have much faith in the
mind-reading abilities of the San Francisco postal service.

February 9, 1961

The birthday surprise for your dad was a complete success
and the pleasure was greatly increased by your phone
call! After a drink at your house we went to the Shadows
for German food, although the cooks were Filipino. After
dinner your brother Don wanted to take your dad to
the Red Garters. The mention of the place brought back
memories of our first date a year ago—the spark that sent
our romance aglowing! That was quite a beautiful evening,
wasn't it?

February 20, 1961

I always seem to miss you most of all each day as the bus
crosses the bay, like right now. The sight at sunset is a
glowing spectacle and the quiet bay waters remind me of
our New Year Eve's cruise in our private "yacht." When
can we do it again?

3. Long-Distance Courtship

The saying "Absence makes the heart fonder" may have been coined by the Roman poet Sextus, who wrote, "Always toward absent lovers love's tide stronger flows." Until the 20th-century creation of the internet and cell phones, there were only two ways for lovers to bridge the distance gap—letters and the telephone. Letters were cheap (a stamp cost four cents in 1960) but the telephone was expensive. There were no free internet conversations capable of connecting two people thousands of miles apart; no FaceTime, no text messaging. I will describe the methods of communication in the 1950s and 1960s for the benefit of my younger readers who were born in the age of email, cell phones, and social media. There were two types of letters: regular and the more expensive air mail. There were two categories of telephone calls: local and long distance. The latter included any call outside the immediate area from which you were calling. All long-distance calls, domestic and international, were placed through an operator, who would make sure the person you were calling answered the phone before connecting you. If it was a collect call, the operator would say, "You have a call from _____. Do you accept the call?" Domestic long-distance calls were very expensive. A call from Janey in Palo Alto, California, to me in Eugene, Oregon, was about $1.00 for three minutes, equivalent to $9.00 in 2021 dollars. My rented apartment in Eugene didn't have telephone service. To call Janey from Eugene, I would have to find a public telephone booth and have a pocket full of quarters. As each three-minute period was coming to an end, the conversation would be interrupted by a pinging sound indicating that it was time to deposit more coins before the call was automatically terminated. It is said that long-distance rates were kept high to cover the cost of providing local service. However, AT&T, originally a subsidiary of the Bell Telephone Company, held a monopoly on telephone service across the country until its breakup in 1984, and the U.S. Government guaranteed its profitability.

Janey's letters about our phone calls reveal how anxious we were about how much they cost and the frustrations of communication and separation in that era, when long-distance lovers might only be able to afford to talk to each other once a month. Telephone calls were so expensive that in her letter below, Janey refers to covering the cost with stock dividends from the family's soy sauce company.

April 4, 1960

Again I have so many things to tell you. I only wish that I didn't have to put it down to paper. I am so tempted to make use of Mr. Bell's invention one of these days. Is there any possible way in which I can contact you? Your office in the biology department? I will soon be coming into a small fortune so I can afford a bit of extra pleasure.

April 23, 1960

You're right about phone calls—we're so pressured for time that nothing comes out very logically. I hope you don't think me too impulsive or irrational for calling you. There are ever so many times in the day that I want to talk to you. Then I can't control myself any longer and must reach for that receiver. Wednesday night I was feeling such happiness and elation that I felt I had to share it with you. "My cup overfloweth."

May 10, 1960

Please don't think me too silly or impulsive for wanting to call you last night. Feelings were built up to a state where I just had to talk to you. But the ironic thing is that the minute I hung up the phone a hundred and one more things had come to mind and the few short minutes simply weren't satisfying enough. I guess we will have to excuse it all to human nature—the more one gets the more one wants.

July 1, 1960
Didn't you find it uncanny how we always get "that" feeling that the other will call? I'm forced to agree with others that love is a strong force. Did you receive any of my thoughts via the mental waves? But don't you find weekends the most difficult time of the week? Then I have more time to myself and thinking and relaxing.

July 20, 1960
Yes, it was so utterly delightful to talk to you last night. To H*** with the phone bill.

August 2, 1960
What a good phone call last night (the door was closed) and it seems that we get more talked over in the last few calls than in some of the earlier ones.

August 3, 1960
Yes, your poster sounds utterly delightful. No doubt it is another expression of your love for marching music. It reminds me that my roommate and I were talking this evening about colors and their relationship to words—how we associate our thoughts in colors, i.e., dream in color. So anyway—when you see "A" don't you automatically visualize red? "B" for blue and "C" for yellow?[4]

Thank you for the article on mountaineering. Gosh, it was beautifully expressed—so unlike ordinary newspaper

---

4 At this point Janey did not yet know that I was colorblind.

writers. I think I can begin to understand your love for that thrilling sport.

August 5, 1960
The first and only time I've called you station to station and you weren't in. The man who answered sounded like a professor and I couldn't get him to understand me. Then a few minutes ago the operator got me to extension 107 first and a young person answered this time. But alas, no Richard.

I was so pleased you returned my call last night. I felt I had to talk to you and was ever so frustrated I didn't get through to you.

August 23, 1960
Your call this evening has kept me up in the "pink" clouds all night. I wonder how I can possibly refrain from hearing your voice more than once a month. But in all practicality and in anticipation of our future together—silence is the battle cry!

September 1, 1960
Already I'm discovering how very difficult it is to keep the promise of not calling. Perhaps thinking about it makes it all the more difficult. Remember spring quarter? When we talked only about once every two weeks and then it was only about three minutes each time? And I keep trying to tell myself this will be the shortest interval that we'll be apart until next July. So if I continue to rationalize my emotions, the time may yet go faster.

September 5, 1960

I was so happy after your call and being able to talk to you as if we were together chatting casually and not 600 miles apart. Don't get angry, but I couldn't resist the temptation and called the operator about the charges on the call. There's no doubt about it, we set a new record: 63 minutes, coming to $15.90 plus 10% tax, $17.50 [$157.50 in 2021 dollars]. Not as bad as I figured it would be. I presume that there must be a lower rate for each additional three minutes. Am I becoming a more and more expensive date? It seems to me that the clock just zooms faster and faster each time we talk to each other. Anyway, I'll not mention cost again because I get so much enjoyment out of our calls.

September 28, 1960

I always feel so rejuvenated each time I talk to you, even though I appear to you to be so nervous! Really not that much, only that I want to cover so much ground in the minimum of time and then hear you talk. Hmm, what a voice—especially when you pick up the phone at the first ring and quietly say, "Biology." Oh what calmness and how official sounding! I love it!

October 2, 1960

After the phone call and having Dad guess that the call was $5.00 [$45 in 2021 dollars] out of his pocket (kidding of course), I made a thorough investigation of phone charges as follows: Person to person $1.40/3 minutes [$12.60]; $.25 each additional minute. Station to station $.90/3 minutes [$8.10]; $.25 each additional minute. I gather these are evening and Sunday rates. So we can easily afford a 10- to 20-minute call once and only once a week? Or very short ones when we feel like it? Agreed? It's not at all fun to be practical, but think of the additional sets of Brastoff china.

October 19, 1960

You're right. No calls until Thanksgiving will never work out. The phone bill for the past month was as bad as last—but my roommate and I nearly collapsed the evening when we saw a bill for $230 for long-distance calls [$2,070 in 2021 dollars] but they had not subtracted the last payment. I'll be solvent next month, so don't even ask the amount of the bill.

October 20, 1960

I have been trying to call you all night but apparently the cards are against me or it simply wasn't meant to be. There is the most obnoxious male operator at the U of O switchboard who refuses to ring the extension unless the caller is certain that there will be someone on the other end of the line expecting the call. Now please try to think of a way to fire him!

I think I will give that operator one more chance to ring your extension, #703. I do so much feel the need to talk to you. Oh, my kite is up in the clouds after talking to you. I feel so relaxed under the influence and spell of your soothing voice.

November 28, 1960

I think we can now force ourselves to outgrow taking the easier way out of the condition of being apart. Practically calculating, at the rate we have been calling, we might well have paid Pacific Telephone and Telegraph close to $1,000 [$9,000] by next March. And that can well be at least enough for half a car. So if we don't get started again during the shorter period apart there is a strong possibility that we might survive if we're silent from January to March.

January 4, 1961

Your call last night was a most wonderful surprise. I had been hoping but didn't dare pick up the phone as it is no longer my own. It's sad that our words are now so expensive these days. I am so looking forward to the day when there'll never be any long separations.

February 26, 1961

After talking to you Friday I was so happy again. I am usually terribly grouchy at the end of the week but the sound of "Biology, Cheu speaking" instantaneously put me in giddish and "higher than a kite" spirits.

Letters

Letter writing is an art form that requires the writer to think about what to write and how to say it in a way that reflects the writer's intent and is understood by the recipient. Writing a letter is hard work, especially if it is about a topic that is emotional for both parties. The length of a letter, whether short or long, is measured in words connected to convey a message that seeks to evoke an equally thoughtful response in the recipient's mind. In the era of letter writing, prior to the age of email, a friend was someone you knew personally—more than today, when the social media connotation of a "friend" is an acquaintance or social contact—and who would come to your assistance if called upon. In other words, a letter is personal.

Janey and I became engaged on June 15, 1960, three weeks before she wrote the first letter below. In the following letters, she expresses a need for two things: private time to think about how she feels about the major changes ahead—marriage, career, lifestyle—and time to discuss these topics together, neither of which were available to the extent she wanted them.

July 3, 1960

I'm at home for the weekend. Mom was considerate and
sent my sister and roommate to the museum so that I
finally can have some privacy to write you some lines.
It amazes me how much I crave some moments alone
to think and to tell you some of the things on my mind.
When living with such a close friend it makes it difficult
to be independent and go off on one's own way at times.
How I appreciate dorm life, where it is a simple matter to
disappear into one's own world and emerge when I feel like
it. My roommate then and I always went our own separate
ways but could nevertheless communicate when we needed
one another.

It has occurred to me that privacy and being alone with
oneself is a very important thing. And don't you think that
it is necessary for married people also? I think of how nice
it is sometimes when we can just sit by each other for long
intervals, not talking, each in our own thoughts yet feeling
the warmth and closeness of the other.

In disguise these few months apart may be a good
thing, giving us a chance to discover more of ourselves as
well as thinking out certain problems more thoroughly,
though I haven't come across anything great yet, thank
goodness. And then we hold what we do have in a more
precious, appreciative way. However, the distance and time
didn't appear so very long until the night I talked to you.

My ears just clung to your words, which brought you closer and back down to reality.

How very tempted I was when my roommate Mary's brother and his wife asked if I wanted to drive up to Oregon this weekend. Then I thought it would be wiser for both of us to catch up on some rest as well as forcing myself to get used to the idea that there will be long months when we are apart.

July 4, 1960
Yes, 550 miles do seem like thousands at times. I'm so glad for Mr. Bell's wonderful invention. He has shrunk some of the miles, even though for only a few minutes, but very wonderful, precious minutes.

July 7, 1960
Why do I get so absolutely tongue tied and stage frightened when I hear you call? How can you imagine just how many things one can say in the span of three minutes?

July 11, 1960
Yes, I think that you calling collect will solve all Bell AT&T problems. I've instructed Mary to accept the calls only when I'm around. I think that will be more economical and alleviate problems of anxiety that the prearranged times can cause. There are times that I feel I simply must talk to you and spontaneous calls are simply more satisfying and more pleasant all the way around. Don't you agree?

October 7, 1960
What would you think if a special delivery package arrived at your door next Thursday morning and it contained me?

Mary is planning to go home next week, and naturally she needs a traveling companion who would only go as far as Eugene. I have decided that it's within budget, and I promise not to disrupt any of your work and be as quiet as a mouse (though not the kind in our lab). I want to see you so badly and it'll be less expensive than two long distance calls, especially the kind we usually make. And don't you want to see me?!!!

October 7, 1960

I hope you're OK with my visit next week via train—and isn't it a good time and opportunity, picnic time?

October 9, 1960

Only four more days. How I like the idea of a spontaneous trip. I just called your dad to tell him of my visiting you and ask if I could bring you any messages. I got just one— the typical one from parents but will save it to deliver personally on Thursday morning.

October 10, 1960

I spent all night thinking of the days that we'll be together—hmm, terribly excited. The Van der Veltes are sweeter than sweet to lend us their auto for the weekend. You indeed have wonderful friends. I am looking forward to dinner with them on Friday. But you'd better keep their little son Gus away from me or else I may start getting fancy ideas about our little Spot.[5]

---

5 The dog in *Dick and Jane*. We playfully called our future child "Spot."

I felt back in Eugene again when I talked to you this evening. It was so hard to step down from this weekend's heaven. Oh, how I hate trains, especially departure and watching your tall, handsome, white-coated figure grow smaller as we pulled away from the station. At that moment I would have given anything to be able to fly off the train. I was so absolutely happy every minute that we were together but just thinking of it and communicating via letters and mental telepathy will pull us through until Thanksgiving, tu ne penses pas?

Particularly, I'm so happy to have gotten a glimpse of your work and the wonderful group of people you associate with. Now I know how strongly you feel about Oregon and especially the opportunities for you there. Yes, it was the wisest decision that you made for your doctorate—that is, unless you decide you want the primates up in Portland. But whatever your final decision, it will be best and I'll be happy so long as I can share it with you.

In the short afternoon visit I grew very fond of the Soderwalls and of course the Van der Veldes are the sweetest and most generous couple. I enjoyed their company immensely. And I hope they will still be there with darling Gus when we move up. Oh dear, I can't help but dream of our marriage together—going to school, cooking your dinner, entertaining our friends, and being so close to you.

October 23,1960

Nosy little Mother of course wanted a detailed account of my visit, including the hour at which you left the motel.

Then she retracted her question, realizing that she was probing in too personal a matter.

While walking in Chinatown with Mom we walked into none other than Dr. Henry Cheu!! Just a brief sidewall conversation but your Dad looked so pleased—he simply lit up and beamed when I spoke of my very nice trip up to see you.

October 24, 1960
Each time I think of the trip to Eugene I see again the tall white-coated figure with his long stride coming to greet me and then waving goodbye again as the train went away.

Janey's mention of the motel where she stayed when she visited me in Eugene reminds me of one of our favorite songs, sung by Frank Sinatra and many others.

"There's a Small Hotel"

I'd like to get away, Junior
Somewhere alone with you
It could be oh, so gay, Junior
You need a laugh
Or two

A certain place I know, Frankie
Where funny people can have fun
That's where the two will go,
Darling
Before you can count up
One, two, three.

For there's a small hotel
With a wishing well
I wish that we were there together

There's a bridal suite
One room bright and neat
Complete for us to
Share together

Looking through the window
You can see a distant steeple
Not a sign of people
Who wants people?

When the steeple bell says,
"Good night, sleep well, "
We'll thank the small hotel
Together
We'll creep into our little shell
And we will thank the small hotel together

—by Lorenz Hart and Richard Rodgers

4. Getting to Know Each Other

Although Janey and I were Stanford students at the same time for two years, we didn't really know each other. We were like ships passing in the night. We occasionally saw each other and chatted briefly, but we didn't date. Janey was aware of where I was on campus—I covered my bike seat with a green shower cap, which she later told me was hilarious. She didn't know I was colorblind. It was only after the fateful New Year's Eve date that we began to get to know each other.

April 4, 1960

I'm so very pleased that you finally dropped your façade for me. It's so very wonderful knowing you. In fact my feeling toward you has really enhanced my thinking and attitudes toward other things—a much happier outlook and understanding in just everything. I guess when one is happy it is so much easier to be kinder to other people as well as want to do things well. In the past my relations with boys have been full of tension and anxiety—my subconscious unwillingness to give and partake. Thus I feel like an object and begin to scheme and plot as a counter action. Or else it would be an attempt on my part to change that person to fit into my way of thinking, sort of as if I'm the great divine messenger, so put me on a pedestal and be enlightened. No more of that. Also, thanks to your teaching, or more like forcing me to relax at Yosemite, I've been taking things more casually and find myself enjoying things so much more.

April 17, 1960

I really hate to admit this, but your words really do have a wonderfully calming effect on me. I usually get rather horrible at the end of the week—tired and edgy. Just your direct and sensible way of saying things and thinking seems to be that pep pill that sets me off on the right track again. I guess it's because I'm not in the habit of letting people know how I feel, and so I just let it well up inside without knowing how to release the tension. Then hearing from you makes the built up irritants appear so silly and insignificant and they simply die on the spot. So lately after a long tense day in the lab I reread your pages on Oregon U. stationery and everything seems to glow again. I must sound overly sentimental or something, but it works wonders.

April 28, 1960

The other day a friend of mine gave me some very acute objective criticisms of myself. It certainly made me stop and think and try some quick reevaluations. It all seemed to boil down to my trying to live up to a certain idealist image, sort of how I think I should be or living up to a certain character I want others to see in me. I guess this is what you term a "façade." Needless to say, when one trusts another, it is so much easier to be honest and sincere. So I guess it is because I trust you so completely that I can be completely uninhibited and truly honest.

May 4, 1960

An even greater happiness today when I received your letter offering your pin. Yes, I do so want to pledge the El Tigre auxiliary. However, being a very sentimental person I would like to receive it personally on June 11th and not have an intermediary postman rob you of your starring performance. I do hope that the five weeks won't make any difference to you. Pin or no pin, I still love you just the same, and I can be true and faithful, etc. until then. But if you really want me to have it now, I'll wear it with much love and pride.

May 5, 1960
I wish that you wouldn't feel so darn apologetic each time you hand out a bit of advice or a suggestion. There is nothing I would like more of. I'm really not as independent as I enjoy thinking I am, and sometimes it's hard to figure something out completely alone. And at times I may not be absolutely convinced, so I enjoy displaying that fighting spirit of arguing. I do like to know what you think.

May 10, 1960
The designer of your art museum would probably turn over in his grave if he discovered that you have turned his architecture into a Mt. Everest.[6] I have tried imagining your scalings—it's hysterical. I'm literally rolling on the floor each time I think of it.

June 4, 1960
Oooh, the roses and the thought behind them are the most beautiful and divine things in this world! You are wonderful! I can't begin to express how upset and dejected I felt after the dreadful four hours of my statistics final exam. I just staggered home with emptiness, literally streaming with tears. Then as I dragged upstairs I detected a box of flowers and I wondered, what lucky girl were they destined for? My curiosity drove me to

6 I was a member of the University of Oregon mountaineering club and an avid mountain climber. I used the façade of the campus art library to practice climbing up a sheer face by myself.

investigate further. I peered nearsightedly, and instantly my tears were transformed into tears of happiness and excitement. Thank you, thank you! You've lifted every single grey cloud and I feel that I can soar through any final, and actually they no longer seem so important or traumatic. Those delicate long-stemmed flowers have conveyed $10^6 + 1$ words of sentiment and filled me with love and joy. Oh, I'm simply floating.

While I and the other girls in the house were exclaiming over the flowers, one girl happened to ask me who this "Dick" was. It turns out that she is an older buddy of yours. Do you remember Sally? She told me all about that hysterical visit of yours to Chicago when you couldn't find the town you were staying in. Sally sends her hellos and said that you are on her list of favorite people. Secret to tell you: you are at the top of mine.

June 25, 1960

I must admit I was impressed. My roommate while scrutinizing the '60 QUAD[7] found that you had managed to sneak into one of the campus shots. And sitting next to Wally [Stanford President Wallace Sterling] no less. Gosh, you still have a hold on this place.

June 26, 1960

Just before I left home tonight Mom started on one of her very infrequent lectures. At the time I felt very antagonistic as usual, but now I'm so very glad that she brought some of my faults to my attention. Mainly, my very unpleasant mannerisms when others' faults annoy me and trying to correct them. I'm very arrogant and

---

7 Stanford's annual yearbook.

domineering, my face screws up and my voice gets very shrill. Gosh, I'm even worse than my cousin. Imagine all the things you'll have to put up with. Well, certain things will have to change even if you don't believe in changing people.

July 3, 1960
Your analogy of marriage and mountaineering was beautiful, dear poet. I agree entirely, especially about pride. In our 20 or so years we have been in the process of building ourselves up as an individual and independent. One often fears that to let another in destroys that status. It all lies in a very delicate balance between being oneself, sharing oneself, and accepting another. But it never ceases to amaze me how easily it seems to come when one is in love.

July 4, 1960
I was rereading one of your letters and came across your comment on the various types of parents you saw on the train to Oregon. I thought about it again when I, my sister, and my roommate were talking over dinner last night, comparing our childhood reactions to our parents—how we feared that our parents would leave us, and there were times when we thought our parents to be so insensitive and inadequate. Now I wouldn't trade them for any other and only hope we can do as good a job. So it is probably also with your dad—though he wasn't particularly interested in your music, he was certainly interested in you as a person, with love and guidance.

I wonder where we started? But I guess being a bit older we were more ready to accept and give more readily. But still after your last trip down I feel even more deeply in love with you and as you said I didn't seem so nervous. I guess at Yosemite I was still distrustful and was on guard in the male-female game. I'd always felt that I was never very skillful at the game and would then fall and hurt myself. I don't let such silly ideas trouble me now.

July 5, 1960
Your weekend sounded so very lovely that I long even more for us to share it together. Your friends seem to be such a happy family. I do hope that I can meet them someday and their little boy.

July 8, 1960
I'm on the train to San Francisco—that slow "milk" train that takes forever to get to the city, over an hour and a half. But it's very relaxing and I also could put this time to good use, writing to you. I had to borrow a pen from the conductor, who was so nice as to also bring me a writing board. Gosh, do I live in style. Mary brought me to the train and also your letter. Thank you for that very charming article—the woman hit upon many important points in a very simple way. I read the other two articles you sent last night. I was particularly impressed by the second article. It was a beautifully painted portrait of the scientist, so much of which you so often talk about.

The ride is very nice today but not quite comparable to the one with you, although I'm sitting in the same seat at the very end of the car. The people outside are all in cotton dresses and short sleeves, little boys running around in T-shirts and jeans, mail trucks bustling efficiently about. Such are the sights as the train plods thru towns and tall eucalyptus groves and miles of suburban-tract homes.

July 12, 1960

"Dearest Richard." Yes, I think that I like "Richard" much better. It reminds me less of our first-grade *Dick and Jane* reader, but whatever name, I do love you just as much as ever.

Gus took his family up to Yosemite for a weekend camping trip. I knew you had picked the perfect time to visit the place. His comments about it brought back the very nicest memories. Unfortunately, they had a very difficult time trying to find an inch of room to pitch camp. After much searching, they found a camp which also allowed pets. It was dirty everywhere, like living in a septic tank. Moral of the story: never go to Yosemite in July. Golly, if I saw it now the sight would probably shatter all the beautiful mental pictures I have of the place.

July 14, 1960

I wish you would clue me in on your secret for getting so much done in one day—watching the convention, reading about Hitler and Stanford alums, making hamster cages, giving lectures. Here I barely get eight hours of work done, cook dinner, and before I know it, it's past 1:00 a.m. and I'm ready for bed.

July 15, 1960

Oh, thank you for the stuffed animal, El Tigre. He's absolutely darling and so apropos. You're too wonderful in thinking of such a delightful surprise. I hold him and think of you.

It sometimes frightens me a bit when I look around and see all the problems that other people have—and things seem to be working out so well for us. Of course there may be minor conflicts, but love will probably just push them aside with the greatest of ease.

July 17, 1960

Right now I'm just counting the days until the 19th of August. I was at the airport yesterday and I thought of the day when I'll be there again waiting for your plane to land. I've promised myself that this time I'll be on time—I'm so determined I'll not be late again. It was most dreadful last time as I flew down Bayshore Highway thinking how forlorn you would be waiting at the deck with no welcoming committee in sight.

Mom and Dad are taking a trip to the Northwest in the early part of August. Told them that I really wanted to go along if they left me off at Eugene. Dad squelched my plans, saying that he has a full car with two extra passengers. But I'm quite sure that they will stop in Eugene for a few hours, and would want to see your hamster cages. No, actually they are probably almost as anxious to see you as I am. Dad is terribly fond of you— he never says much, but you should see his eyes light up whenever I mention your name.

July 19, 1960

I couldn't wait to gave Mary her birthday gift last night—a pair of long sliver ear rings—and today I told her it was also part of your gift. She sends her thanks. It was so sweet and thoughtful of you to think of my roomie's birthday. As for the cost of the gift, it was a most nominal sum. So why don't you just give me an extra call someday or just talk about three more minutes?

July 20, 1960

You certainly hit the nail on the head when you attributed our childhood training to the Chinese Golden Rule.[8] In this instance, that is when our American nationalism (is "influence" a better term?) breaks down. But that is the part of my training that I am most proud of. I wasn't aware of it so much until I entered college and lived with other girls in the dorm. I find that it gives one a happier and more serene attitude toward life. Then also it may be simply love in the family that stabilizes our emotions and allows us to view the world under a beautiful light. It pleases me so that our basic ideas on the subject are in equal accord. How wonderful it would be to put it into practice with our own children.

What's really nagging on my nerves now are the newsletters I must write for the Chinese Students Conference. They have been on the agenda for weeks and as usual I've procrastinated. Somehow I cannot seem to get enthusiastic about the conference. Perhaps it's rebelling against the position of secretary, which is always inevitably conferred upon me. Really I detest any sort of writing—except of course writing to you. Yes, communicating with you in any way is always so satisfying.

July 24, 1960

Oh, I just remembered something and dashed down to the library to pick up a chemistry text to check chromium's place in the electromagnetic series. It wasn't there. Were you trying to conceal something else?[9]

---

8 "Do not impose on others what you do not wish for yourself."
9 Picking up the chemistry text reminded Janey that I graded my dates using the energy levels of the chemical elements in the periodic table. She's wondering if I

July 26, 1960

Your picture is before me as I write. Wow, what a rugged mountaineer!! That open shirt effect . . . ohhhh! Having a photo of you brings me miles closer to you, it seems. Memory is nice but it can play such devilish tricks.

July 26, 1960

But 0.9+ (Chromium)[10] . . . umph! That's absolutely crushing. No, it's rather amusing—very glad you told me of it.

July 28, 1960

Your mountaineering last weekend [in eastern Oregon] truly sounded like a wonderful experience. But it still seems to me to be quite a precarious sport. Do they ever take women along? A taste of it might alleviate my mind. I don't relish the idea of leaving women and children down at the bottom for a picnic. That reminds me of the stories of the wars in medieval Europe when the women and children often sit at the edge of the battlefield eating lunch, etc. while the men are in combat. I can't understand how they can possibly digest their food. But then, I gather it's no worse than eating peanuts at a football game.

September 1, 1960

I think, Richard, that I would like to see you get your master's early—but that's because of the very selfish reason of wanting you to be working nearby. However, I don't think it would be fair to you or our future if you don't feel that you have a firm knowledge of basic biology and that you want to do that before you go ahead on your PhD.

---

had a secret code hidden in the book.
10 Another reference to my using the Periodic Table to rate my dates.

That additional month may prove more valuable other than from the monetary standpoint. The extra money that you make in those months will probably not make any difference when you look in retrospect a few years hence. Anyway, Richard, do whatever you think would be best.

August 3, 1960
Richard dear, do take good care of yourself. Your schedule sounds absolutely hectic and you seem to have your hands in everything.

August 6, 1960
Oh, your prof just infuriates me. I wish I could do something to knock him off his high horse that plods along aimlessly. I have the impression from your letters that he's a Dr. Page[11] type of person but without so much enthusiasm. It certainly must be frustrating working for someone like that who doesn't back up his own men. And it is a shame through no fault of his that you people can't hire an engineer or even a handyman to do the things that you do. No doubt you have better things to work on than just merely building hamster cages. But then again, even a menial task as that can bring you much insight on laboratory equipment. You handled the situation beautifully, with great finesse. I'm just beginning to see all the helpful hints I've picked up bleeding mice in our little plastic animal bleeder.

August 6, 1960
I honestly don't see how your prof expects you to be doing ten different things at once. Something has to be sacrificed

---

11 I was Dr. Page's teaching assistant at Stanford.

and it disturbs me that you have to do so much of the handy work when you have so much research and reading awaiting. I am very glad though that you held your temper.

August 8, 1960

I do find the Leroy Anderson music most charming. That's the type of thing that always manages to put me in a gay and carefree frame of mind. However, there's still nothing that has the same effect on me as the music from *Pal Joey*, which sends me to no end.

When I got home last night Mary wanted to see *Never So Few*. (Remember our first and only movie date? What element did I get that time on your file card?) So we packed our pillows and blankets and headed for the drive-in again.

August 10, 1960

But as I said on the phone, the first thing we must get before all else is a meat grinder. Oh, I felt as if I've chopped enough meat tonight for the entire Chinese Army, although most of it got splattered all over me and the kitchen. I do enjoy cooking Chinese food and it's wonderful knowing that not too long from now I will be cooking for you.

Thank you muchly for giving us music again with a transistor radio. Mary's so exulted that she won't have to listen to my off-key singing anymore. You do have the most perfect ideas. But what will you do without music in your office to keep you cheerful when you work?

August 15, 1960

I've been thinking and have come to the conclusion that true happiness in life is love, especially being so completely in love with you. And I do feel we do have a most beautiful relationship. It has also occurred to me how very much alike our temperaments really are. When I'm under stress to get thigs done, any little thing that comes in the way is almost a traumatic experience in my own mind. But the feeling blows away very quickly when I have some time to think. Oh, Richard, can you visualize all the things you will have to put up with in me? Are you sure you can bear it?

August 17, 1960

I do hope that my comment on the phone last Monday didn't upset you too much or set you thinking about other problems. It'll just have to be a matter of finding the best compromise—which won't be too taxing to make. More when I see you.

Yesterday I got wondering whether you could possibly put up with a grouchy wife in the morning and a grouchy wife when you get home for dinner. These are the times I go into long silences until the coffee wakes me up finally.

I guess I was just very tired last night. I'm taking your advice and go scuttling down and around the lab in my swivel chair or high stool. Promise to take it very easy for the next two days so you will be completely rested for the wonderful weekend (when you are here from Eugene). I have been looking forward to it for so long. Gus said I could take Monday off.

You know, I carry all your letters in my huge basket until, of course, it gets overloaded, and then they get filed away. It's so wonderful to be able to pull out your sweet dear words and read them until they are nearly memorized down to the last word. Each time I read your letters I feel warm and so happy again, no matter how ghastly the rest of the world is.

September 1, 1960

Hmm, I'm glad you like Tchaikovsky's 5th symphony also. It's one of the few well-worn recordings we have at home. The jazz station we have been picking up is getting better and better. Especially since they include some of my favorites as well as interspersing the program with classical pieces.

I'm hoping the latest CARE package arrives in good condition. The lady at the store told me to inform the recipient that nothing can harm it, although the heat may make the things look rather messy. And don't worry about the bacteria or mold. They only enhance the flavor, though not the appearance. So, dear gourmet, have fun!

September 1, 1960

Although I live for letters from you, I worry so when they are dated at 2:55 in the morning.

September 12, 1960

I'm very glad to hear that Montgomery Ward has equipped you so well for the rain. Did you also get a green shower cap for the seat of your bike? That's how I remembered you when you were going to school down here, always racing down the Quad as fast as anyone could pedal on a black bike with a green shower cap. Yes, I was particularly impressed by the ingenuity. Except it did use to disturb me when this boy would never stop long enough before he was off again like a streak of lightning. Yes, how ironic that now it is a near impossibility to get us off the phone even though it's long distance.

September 24, 1960

I'm still in the clouds of those heavenly six days when you were home. Hmm, but there were some hectic moments of stress, i.e., no key to the gas cap. Despite everything, especially having people around at every turn, those were indeed too wonderful for words days. Now I will begin counting the shopping days until Thanksgiving.

In spite of my ripe old age of 22 years I've still not seen snow fall. Is there a possibility that we might go up to see the snow? No, on second thought, I get cold too easily. Perhaps sitting by a warm fire together is a more comfortable idea.

September 25, 1960

Living at close quarters with anyone for a long period can start grinding on one's nerves. Last Friday, the taut nerves exploded, precipitated by my accidentally dropping a can of tuna on Mary's toes. I admit I never sound very sorry in such situations because I never quite know what to do—kiss toes? And in fact find it halfway humorous that my aim was so good. Then I got upset over another thing, and you have never heard such a silent household in Palo Alto. Oh, I'm impossible when I get angry but must learn to be more understanding and forgiving. Stubborn me can keep up a curtain of silence for months but decided it's absolutely stupid causing much more pain. In our case, I hope you will always tell me what troubles and disturbs you.

September 27, 1960

Enclosed is an article ["The Lab Coat as a Status Symbol"] that Anna sent to Mary. I thought it was very pertinent to you and your field. Particularly amusing are the lines underscored in red.

September 28, 1960

In case you don't know, I've even learned how to make curtains. Didn't you ever notice those lopsided straggly things hanging in our living room? Those were my first attempt and I had to rush them in time for a party. Oh well, they keep the flies out and provide a nook for Mom to hide behind when spying on the actions of her children.

I spent ages grocery shopping. I love the process of slowly surveying the new products and exotic foods, new T.V. dinners to laugh at, etc. And did you know they now have macaroni in the shapes of space men and wagon wheels?[12]

October 1, 1960

I didn't mean to cause you so many palpitating moments with my teasing. But I do enjoy a bit of teasing one I love, namely such a darling fiancé, and I typically like to see that smile and hear you laugh.

October 5, 1960

I've started in with your Faulkner book *Light in August*. I'm impressed with his very sensitive and poetic style. Thank you for the recommendation. I also have read a couple of chapters of *Flight* which is, as you've said, very apropos and perceptive.

October 7, 1960

Yes, I adore liverwurst. It almost stands side by side with

---

12 Janey brings this to my attention because I was a biology intern in the Mercury space program at Holloman Air Force Base in the summer of 1959.

cheese. Following your routine, we have been buying cheese in huge two-pound chunks. And we have gotten terribly fond of Oregon Tillamook, being zesty. Once I get started on the stuff I can't stop.

October 17, 1960
I agree that the short weekend has brought us a great deal closer.

October 26, 1960
I'm so very excited that you are looking over Dr. Pickering's lab setup at Stanford. From what you have said, it sounds terribly interesting. Then again, I do like what you have at the U. of O. Well, how does it feel, young man, to have to make decisions?

October 31, 1960
A very domestic day today spent entirely on working on your surprise. Mary and I brought our work with us—we're inseparable from our knitting now! I'm so anxious to get it finished in time for you to fight the cold weather with it. But at the rate I am going the surprise might not be ready until summer sets in. However, each stitch is engraved with my love for you so even if it doesn't fit at all, I expect you to appreciate it nevertheless.

I didn't get to bed as early as planned. I got involved in a chess game with Mary and then knitting between moves, a very productive way to spend time, keeping hands and mind busy all the time (I'm of the type who can never sit still anyway.)

I got such a thrill reading your letter today describing Dr. Kezar. I'm so proud that you want to be an enthusiastic as well as intelligible-to-audience type of teacher. And do you remember our very first meetings together were that of a teacher-student relationship? The very first time was my chemistry and then later in the library when I trapped you in the reserve book room to help me with my music. Even those days when we weren't on the best of terms I still considered you a savior in many of my impossible courses. Amazing, but only after talking to you did I finally understand the material. Getting back to Dr. Kezar, I would like very much to meet him. He sounds quite a lot like Gus, who always attacks everything with great enthusiastic vigor.

November 2, 1960

Tonight I made an important decision: Richard, you simply have to expand a few inches—chestwise, that is. After getting to where the armholes start, I thought I should count the number of stitches I had, and to my horror, I discovered that I, not being the best mathematician, started off with ten too many stitches, making the sweater two inches too wide in the front. Didn't you say that you didn't mind baggy sweaters? I want you to look simply superb in it, as you looked when I got off the train three weeks ago and saw you in a white raincoat and corduroy jacket.

November 7, 1960

The charts you prepared for your seminar were absolutely beautiful. Your seminar must have surpassed all those I heard when I was up at the U. of O. I wish I could have heard you speak. I'm just bursting with pride over your excellent work.

I hope that talk with the Upjohn pharmaceutical company has turned you away from thoughts of being a salesman. I just know that you will be so much happier being a $6,000 a year professor than a $12,000 a year drug peddler. And I can be happy without Christian Dior clothes—so long as I can make my own copies.

November 8, 1960
Thinking of you . . . the rabble rouser, part crusader, especially the one who actually goes out and gets things accomplished. One thing is certain, there'll never be a single dull fraction of a second being married to you.[13]

November 15, 1960
That was indeed a profitable visit to the U. of O. medical school Saturday, even if you had not heard any papers. And I can well imagine how impressive the place and the people were. I'm very glad you are looking into other possibilities for doctorate work, for it gives you a better idea of what's happening in research in general. I guess you now face the dilemma of too many choices. It's a big decision—even greater than that of marrying me because it now involves several more people, including our future children, Spot and Puff. I wish you were here now and could explain it all to me in detail, that is, what fields you are interested in and how you might attack them. But I guess my patience will have to wait until Thanksgiving, only one week away.

I was a delinquent today. I woke up this morning and decided that I was too tired and my throat was a bit dry

---

13 Janey told her friends that she was marrying a "Crusader Rabbit," a popular cartoon of the era depicting a character who ran around trying to do heroic things.

87

(more psychosomatic, I think) to go to work. I do feel a bit guilty as the people in the lab were so sorry that I felt so poorly. In fact Avril Mitchison walked down twice to Mary's office to leave me messages of sympathy and get-well wishes. But the last one superseded them all: "Tell Janey not only to get well soon but come back quickly as I can't do anything without her." Great ego booster!

Yesterday I finished off all the remaining experiments and even found time to clean the lab from top to bottom, including the incubator caked with rat and mice fecal materials. We've run out of antigen and most things are at a standstill.

November 28, 1960
How could I possibly fall asleep while you were talking Saturday night? It proves, however, that your voice is indeed soothing.

I'm so happy we had such a revealing talk Saturday night. I think I really am beginning to understand the man I will marry. And thank you for your understanding.

I have been thinking about our personalities and how much we are alike in being "outer directed." We were discussing a related subject in the lab today, very much in the general vein of what we talked about Saturday. Gus brought out an acute comment, that it is very natural for humans' natures to be concerned about how we want to impress others, but the importance is that we realize this fact and make an attempt to put it in its proper perspective and not let it dominate us.

December 13, 1960
In a sense I am glad to get back to Palo Alto and start

feeling independent again. It's always warm to go home but I feel so guilty with Mom and Dad pampering me so, which is very nice until I think that in six months I'll be married and in a few short years may even have Spot and Puff to care for.

January 5, 1961
You were so right about our trusting one another more. We aren't afraid to shout at one another or show our temper. (Hmm, mine is very vicious, n'est-ce pas?)

January 8, 1961
Curious me found it very exciting to discover new parts of Richard I had never known—the methodical Richard who does things step by step, keeping a record of nearly every word written and spoken. I was particularly amused at your saving every little bit and scrap of paper. (Hmm, what a bonfire.)

February 1, 1961
Enclosed is an article I found this morning: "A Matter of Taste. How to Choose a Bottle of Wine without Opening It":

Champagne is for weddings—perhaps the first wine the young couple has ever tasted is the champagne bridal cup— but it is not always suitable for the less exalted celebrations after the wedding is over. Champagne is too costly, too ostentatious, to serve to your husband's boss, your brother-in-law or the couple next door. Occasions of this sort call for a bottle of excellent dry dinner wine. But how can you choose such a wine? . . . There is an almost infallible method of making sure that the bottle you take home from the store contains wine that is at least excellent and possible superlative, without even touching its cork; you ask the bottle questions and the bottle answers you.

—*Mademoiselle*, February 1961

February 20, 1961
One of the most wonderful things about having you back on March 20th will be the end of communicating by mail. Don't think that I don't like to write you; it's just my most ineffective way of transmitting thoughts and nothing ever sounds the same on my paper. Will you be glad to see the end of Sody's[14] old typewriter and buying ribbon after ribbon?

February 21, 1961
Today I thought back on our courtship. About every little time we were together before the pinning and engagement! And how strange emotions are—I felt I barely knew you, yet more than anything else I knew I wanted to be your wife. I feel that's the greatest miracle in my 22 years!

February 26, 1961
I've been thinking about ways to shorten the wait of the three weeks and it struck me that it would be easiest if we didn't think of it in terms of the number of days. We have to reconsider Mrs. Wilbur's[15] wise advice and take things as they come, one step at a time, and before you know it, you'll be home and the oral exams will be left behind.

Don't let my inquiries into your progress on that paper

14 Dr. Soderall, my advisor. I typed letters to Janey in his office.
15 Ruth Wilbur was my mentor in high school. She was the daughter-in-law of Dr. Ray Lyman Wilbur, Stanford University president and Secretary of the Interior in the Hoover administration.

"shake you up"! I do trust your judgement and discretion in doing what's most important at this time. So don't let the minor details disturb your peace of mind. But be certain to relax—tension is your mortal enemy now, so it's absolutely necessary to completely squelch him.

March 2, 1961

In a few more hours I should be in Oregon. I am so thrilled and excited. I'm so glad we decided on the trip. However, no plane leaves for Oregon Friday night so I have to take a West Coast plane which leaves San Francisco at 8:00 a.m. Saturday morning and arrives in Eugene around 10:30 a.m. That will cut off our weekend but it's so much better than nothing at all. Also, you can have all of Friday to study a bit, as it's illogical to think that you wouldn't be distracted with me around.

March 12, 1961

On the way home today, I went through the park where the traffic was heavy and I took what appeared to be the closest exit. Instead of an exit it wound around and around into parts that were more like the wilderness than Golden Gate Park. We must explore this section of the park as soon as you get home. So beautiful and romantic!

5. What Will I Do after I Graduate from Stanford?

The letters below show Janey struggling to figure out the direction of her studies and her career after her graduation from Stanford, and how she will manage her career and her role as a wife. Her first letter below mentions Chicago. We lived in Chicago for two years while I was working on my MBA at Northwestern University's Kellogg School of Management. We lived in one of the poorest neighborhoods of the city with three very young children. We barely survived on our savings and my salary as the evening cashier at Trader Vic's restaurant at the Palmer House hotel. Janey's close friend also lived in Chicago with young children and a husband doing his medical residency; they were equally impoverished. All of us, adults and children, survived our rite of passage in Chicago to go on to more pleasant adventures.

January 26, 1960

Have you ever heard about any good grad schools with microbiology departments? My advisor is truly the most helpful man. I'm saying this a bit sarcastically. When I asked him for some suggestions, he told me to just pick out a city where I would like to live and then write to the university there. Honestly, I do think that I'm more interested in what the school has to offer than just the external surroundings. But I was grateful to him for the advice about Chicago. He said whatever I do, never live in Chicago, it's utterly horrible.

February 17, 1960

Oh, the GRE was just the most impossible test ever! The moment I looked over the questions on the exam I saw all my chances of going to grad school go out the window. I had hoped to really impress the professor on the test, as he is head of the department, quite a renowned immunologist, who could give me a good recommendation. But now, it would certainly be rather presumptuous of me to even approach him. I have been sneaking around the department like a hunted fugitive these days, so very ashamed to even show my shadow. It's utterly depressing.

Many thanks for sending those announcements and good advice. I do see what you mean after talking to some of the grad students in my classes. They too seem to be just wandering around, exploring and experiencing. For so long, I had the idea that after four years of college one should know definitely what one wants to do and how to go about pursuing it. Now it appears that the four years are just a stepping stone that has many paths.

It must be such a wonderful thing to actually be sure of what one wants. I know you have that secure inspired feeling. You certainly radiated with it when I last talked to you this vacation time.

I have sort of gotten into some of the research on my paper. I find myself enjoying the detective work to no end. It's one of the most wonderful learning experiences. So I find myself loving my department more and more. Nevertheless, sometimes I still wonder if this is exactly what I want to do. It's so easy to be carried off quite hypnotically into a very specialized, theoretical world that one's department is concerned with, leaving behind the former desires and aspirations. Perhaps it's the problem of taking what opportunity comes along, it being the easiest.

This may sound pretty much insane to you, but I'm anxious to work closely with the medical world, i.e., going off to Formosa to help save people infected with cholera, dysentery, and T.B. It may seem that I'm taking up the sword of the crusader or martyr, but doesn't it seem exciting??? Seriously though, I saw a travelogue on Formosa at the Chinese Club New Year's open house which was purely propaganda, but the strength and bravery of those people really impressed me. And so pompous me thinks that she can offer some type of service. So probably I will end up giving thousands of injections a day, testing blood samples, etc. But how much better it would be than an eight-to-five job over here doing the same! Gosh, all this probably reeks with idealism. Dad thinks so anyway. He thought and felt so in his younger days until he went over to China during the war. He came back pretty frustrated, annoyed, and depressed over the whole situation there. Don't you think that it's very important for one to go through with it—to satisfy all drives, curiosities, etc.?

I have recruited one compatriot on this expedition. You'll never guess who it could possibly be. Yes, my roomie. In fact, she has just sent off some inquiries for us. However, I really don't know enough about anything to do one darn thing, except to bleed rabbits, and that I still don't do very successfully (the poor things about die from shock when I get through with them). That's why I still want to get into grad school and sort of discover what can be done. It's really too bad that enthusiasm doesn't carry one through school grade-wise. And the problem also is that I got too overconfident after doing the best that I have ever done last quarter, especially along with the idea that I was competing with honest-to-goodness medical students. Oh, did that go to my head! But now when I look back on it, perhaps they really weren't so high and mighty after all. Rather a crushing thought!! There is little time to do it in. So at times, it's rather depressing especially with those hundreds and hundreds of stupid lab reports that are so long and routine. That's probably why I dread the thought of being just a lab tech, when the field of research is so fascinating and exciting.

February 26, 1960

Your letter just exploded my little toy balloon I had been waving around like a young child. It has certainly forced me to back down to look again on reality and myself. Thank you. But even looking at reality has not crushed my desires to work in the Orient. Perhaps not immediately, but sometime in the near future. I am beginning to realize that whatever I take on will require patience besides that "driving force" and as you put it, having the "proper equipment" to handle the situation. I guess it is also important to accept certain things which are not the most pleasant, like long dreary lab reports. But I still maintain that lab reports, at this stage of the game, are a regimented exercise of parroting the same concepts over and over again. They also require so much time (because I am so slow) that there is little time left for more interesting investigation into the matter. Furthermore, labs are so planned that they leave little room for one to even make mistakes (i.e., counting the number of bacteria in a phagocytic cell.) But they say one has to begin from the basics for that foundation of knowledge—only I rebel when I have to write volumes on what appears to be the most obvious and simple.

You are so right about learning about what is needed and how to go about getting it. Things in the past have just simply presented themselves on a silver platter. And all I ever had to do was to accept them without really ever taking an active role. In a way I must have thought that enthusiasm and desire were in themselves enough for anything, and a place would be ready and waiting when I said the word.

As for saving lives, I didn't mean in a Florence Nightingale type of crusade. For me, it is more of a feeling of distributing new technological knowledge a bit more widely. Surely the advances of research today will contribute to the future, but the question is, who will get the benefits? First of all, that small island off the coast of China cannot afford it, and its own people in research, etc. are looking for places which can give them better equipment and a more comfortable life.

I have been discovering more and more possibilities in microbiology. It's more vast than I had ever imagined. Now to sit down and look closely into them. It makes me mad when I get so bogged down by the immediate school work that I haven't begun to check on so many things. So I will get down to business when finals are over in two weeks.

March 7, 1960
On a happy note, I just received word this morning from Harvey Hall, who informed me that my department has accepted me for grad work. So if other schools don't want me, I can still return to the "Farm" next fall.

March 28, 1960
I am in Memorial Auditorium anxiously waiting to register for the last time. Such a strange feeling as this ritual has become ever so much a routine. I was holding my breath for fear of the sight of the grades. I couldn't help but feel extremely ashamed of myself for allowing the term

papers to slide through as they did. But it appears that my professors were either very lenient or sympathetic or something, and a 3-point GPA came up again. Oh, I am so thankful. It would be so depressing to have to send my very poor transcript without any good marks to balance out the past (especially winter quarter junior year) to prospective hospitals and grad schools.

April 17, 1960
I drove up early to San Francisco and took the long way home, stopping at the Letterman Hospital to see about the lab tech training there. Thanks to my habitual procrastination, I discovered that they had just made their selection for trainees. However, this time it wasn't entirely my fault. I had talked to some nincompoop some weeks ago who assured me that he would send me the application and I had until the end of April. So that sort of ends hopes to intern at a nationally accredited place. Perhaps there may be some hospitals down in the peninsula as I sort of want to live away from home. And the more I think about it, the more I think it is wise to get some insight into the clinical end of things—that gives one a much better overall perspective as in research labs things can become rather limiting, even though there is so much to learn. Whereas a research technician can't do any diagnostic type of work in hospitals, etc. It would be perfect if a six-month program can be found—I would hate to wait too long before grad school. All I seem to know about is immunology and bacteria. I suddenly felt that way during the Transplantation Seminar. I was really lost when they started talking about embryology and trophoblast cells. However, I was not the only one in that

position—the doctor on the panel requested the definition of "immunologic tolerance," which was the subject he was to comment on. However, I can envisage the amount of immunology I'll be getting at Stanford grad school.

I am finding it very educational to grade papers. I was very impressed with some of the problems that the students discussed in the lab reports. They told me so much I didn't know. The most amusing thing I came across was in the lab assignment which required people to examine a smear from their teeth. One girl found many spirochetes, which she identified as Treponema pallidum. Little did she know that this is the causative agent of syphilis. I think my comment will cure her of being so presumptuous in trying to identify a bacteria from simply a stained smear.

April 23, 1960
There is a possibility that I may be doing my clinical lab tech training at Sequoia Hospital in Redwood City. I hope that the state requirements will let me off after six months as the only course I'm lacking is parasitology. Otherwise the training will be one year. And the thought of an apprenticeship for one year at $200 a month—that type of lab training isn't particularly interesting when it has to stretch out for 12 months. Not to sound conceited, but I think that my background in the field is better than many people's, and most of the program will be repetitious. Nevertheless, a clinical background will be very useful and will help me decide on exactly what phase of lab work I really want to do when I start on grad work.

I was utterly panicked when I received word from the children's hospital in San Francisco informing me that their quota had already been filled. I called the place in Redwood City in desperation and they said that they had two places but were interviewing two other students that day. They said I could talk to another doctor that day. So yesterday I flew down to El Camino. It was the funniest interview I've ever had in my life. They didn't even bother to ask me about anything or to see my transcript. I guess the name "Stanford" does it every time. That doc I saw didn't seem to know anything about the program but simply said that I could train there if I wanted to and they proceeded to take me to the head of the lab and show me around. So I guess that will be one possibility for July 1st.

It will be a hard decision if the job in the Genetics Department comes through. Dr. Lederberg still doesn't know I'm working there part-time as he's been in Europe for some meeting where his wife is presenting a paper. He's the blocking force as of now. I would hate to leave Dr. Nossal in the lurch if he needs an assistant, for Dr. Mitchison has been so good and patient with spastic me.

April 28, 1960

I just received a phone call from the head of labs at the children's hospital in San Francisco. It seems they have an opening in their training program after all. That place may be much better than the one in Redwood City—the RC one turns out to be more of an apprenticeship type of training instead of a real training school with classes and lectures. That's probably why they pay about $50 more and don't screen their applicants so thoroughly.

May 15, 1960

As for after graduation, I am quite positive that I'll be

continuing on with the Genetics Department until about January. There will be so much exciting work there this summer, mostly on problems of transplantation, that the opportunity is too good to pass up, whereas I can get lab tech training anytime. I also feel that some insight into the research world will be more important before I start grad school. Then in January I can start the clinical or public health training if I'm still interested. Right now I'm not quite sure yet. I want to get both in somehow before I go further in school. As you said, I won't be satisfied until I see what the clinical stuff is all about. You're right!!

May 19, 1960

A grad student in microbiology who worked for two years as a lab tech gave me the entire grand tour of the private clinical labs, hospital labs, and public health labs of the San Jose area. I realized that this was the tour I should have taken long ago. "Action" was the word at the hospital, but just the opposite at the public health lab. I wasn't too impressed with the work at the clinic. It's really work there, just chaotic routine and nothing else. At the public health place there seemed to be more opportunity to do things on one's own, a lot of room for exploration.

June 4, 1960

The first thing to do after that test today was to destroy every last stitch of statistics. I've never been so upset with myself as when I couldn't get that concept of "decision theory" correlated in my mind so that it would make statistics more sensible. Maybe I'm dreaming that I can ever really grasp and relate those concepts. It sort of makes graduation seem not quite right. I must retrieve those notes now. When I look back on the past four years and begin comparing, I can honestly say that this year has been the most rewarding, primarily because of my department. And it was really by accident that I stumbled into it. Even up until last year I really had no idea what a microbiologist did. I guess the idea of white lab coats was appealing. Now there seem to be so many things that I would enjoy exploring.

I must remember to talk to Dr. Raffel to see if I can postpone entrance into grad work until the fall of '61. I was amazed when they said that 23 people applied to the department, and because of the sudden upsurge in students they only accepted nine. Sort of bloats my ego. However, I still haven't heard from the public health people confirming the job starting January. They gave me several choices and alternatives and asked me to list my preferences. But I only gave my first choice, that I wanted to work at least six months in the Genetics Department, and then six months with the public health people at Berkeley will give me a public health certificate. From talking to the grad student who had one it appears that it would be more valuable than just a lab tech license. As I mentioned before, after seeing lab techs at work I decided that even one day at it would be just too much. Also that setup at the state public health microbiologist training program with the virus lab seems rather impressive, so by the time the training ends I would just about be ready for fall quarter on the Farm again.

June 6, 1960

Unbelievable—only one more final to go. Whoosh. I just don't know how to react. I am simply numb. It was a strange finals week—I have never gone into the tests so cold. Everyone is packing and leaving. I will be thinking of you when you take your last test!

July 29, 1960

The Public Health people answered more rapidly: yes. I finally answered their 5/20/60 letter, and they still have a position open for me in January. Also, they have another in February. The February one may be better after all. It ends in July, so I can work another month in the lab.

August 5, 1960

Yesterday was a dual purpose trip. First I went over to Berkeley to confirm the public health training. In actuality, it was unnecessary. That is, they didn't tell me any more about the training than before, and furthermore I still have to confirm my acceptance in writing. So I'll be embarking on something new starting January 2. I will certainly hate to leave the atmosphere of our lab, but as you've mentioned, there is a limit to what I can do and learn. Injecting mice will get a bit tiresome by January. But then the mice will leave when the "mice man," Mitchison, returns to Scotland.

At the interview I went with the department head for coffee down in the public health labs. What a difference in attitudes and personalities among the workers. However, the atmosphere immediately changed when it consisted primarily of women. At coffee break the girls were seen to be poring intently over the latest fashion magazines. Down on the Farm, Gus and Ollie probably don't even see their coffee unless it's set down before them and the steam from the coffee begins to fog up the microscope lens so much that they can't work any further. But all in all the public health people were very nice and pleasant (and Miss French flaunted the name "Stanford" everywhere we went to visit). As Connie says, working anywhere can be interesting because there is always an element of humanity there.

September 10, 1960
Your talk with Novick the U. of O. microbiologist has certainly gotten me very excited. His interests (from your excerpts) are not the same as what I'm doing now—the Lederberg domain is upstairs. However, I have been exposed to some in my classes—Bacterial Physiology and Viruses. But it seems that there will be a great deal of room for flexibility. Then again, I wonder if I can be a school girl again and still be a good wife at the same time. I have to weigh it against being a working wife, where I may start feeling stagnant intellectually.

My eavesdropping ears dropped into a short conversation between Mitchison and S. She is working with her husband, who is a professor in the department. She never finished college but she's one of those few rare self-taught women. But now she is beginning to feel the professional chasm between herself and hubby, especially when he goes off to meetings, etc.

No, I would never want us to work as a husband-wife biologist team and turn into the Lederbergs, etc. But I do want to be able to understand what you do and be filled with the appropriate cocktail talk when we have our colleagues over. Seriously, though, I do want to learn merely for a sense of personal intellectual satisfaction. I can't have people thinking that you married a stupid girl who spends her days injecting mice.

Many thanks for the very exciting news about the Novick domain. I mentioned the possibility of studying with Novick to Dr. Mitchison, who got more excited than I. He said it was "jolly nice." He then proceeded to clue me in on Novick's work. I first asked him what he knew about Novick, and then after telling me about permease and adaptive enzymes and E. coli, he wondered why I was so nosy. I felt so reassured when Mitchison showed such pleasure in my desire for more school. Oh, a great sense of security.

September 12, 1960

But Richard, there is a slight worry (I am keeping calm): how can I possibly get into grad school if I have to take that College Record test? I know absolutely nothing about basic biology. In microbiology, the only requirements were the bare minimum that the pre-meds took. I even failed to take the 20 pre-med biology classes except for comparative anatomy, which I skimmed through by the skin of my teeth. And I'm sure they don't include any microbiology questions in those tests. So perhaps you should begin asking Novick if he needs any more lab techs.

September 24, 1960

The med students are returning en masse for the fall quarter. I sort of feel my privacy here being invaded, but then also, I wish that I too were starting school. I'm very

happy that you do want me to do grad work. I do so hope
that it can be arranged and managed. I am most excited.

October 2, 1960

I am still not sure what I should do after December. Much
of it depends on Mary's plans. However, it would still
be best that I continue with Gus even if I live at home.
Commuting each day wouldn't be too bad if I can get hold
of a car. Or else, start looking for a new roomie.

October 19, 1960

How could you possibly think that I would devote
everything to a career in biology if I go to grad school and
give up my most important career, you? Yes, I have that
drive to want to do things well, but wanting to be a good
wife to you overshadows everything else down to the size of
an ant. I just thought that my being able to attend school
would make me a happier person and halfway bearable
to live with, instead of simply a grouchy, tired working
wife after eight hours. With a schedule such as yours as a
student, my being a student would indeed make it easier
to arrange my life around yours. And very important is
my wanting to learn more about many things. Perhaps it
will be best to wait and see how things will work out and
then go at them. It's sort of useless to hash over a problem
over and over again even before knowing whether they'll
consider me as a grad student or provide some financial
assistance. Let's sit tight?

October 31, 1960

Being a stranger or visitor at Guthrie dorm last night
was a strained situation. There apparently is no picking

up from where one leaves off. Even in a matter of months there have been so many changes in all of us. Friday night, Mary and I drove through campus to survey the homecoming floats, which brought back many nostalgic memories. Strangely enough though, when we were in school neither of us paid any attention to such activities, claiming that they were a waste of time. Then when we became alums—oh what hypocrites.

January 5, 1961
I have been giving Lil and Don's suggestion[16] some thought and decided that it's a possibility that shouldn't be left out. But if given a choice I would prefer that you get that PhD as soon as possible. In essence that would mean my having to work for a shorter time. The actual reason I dislike work so much, I've concluded, is having to get up so early and following rigid schedules. Without that it would be great fun.

February 3, 1961
I take back my statement about wanting to be in your lab—that lab assignment is monotonous, especially for the lazy person!

February 21, 1961
How ego inflating that both Gus and Av recommended me to Novick. But you didn't qualify it as to what my position was to be—student or technician? A great difference, as you well know. However, I've been thinking about school today and concluded that public health as it stands now has immense possibilities to offer (perhaps more so since

16 My brother and sister-in-law wanted Janey to work for a year to earn money before we got married instead of entering the public health training program, which did not pay anything. Fortunately, she didn't listen to them.

I'm just starting in training) and there is a lot that I
have to catch up on before I can even start grad work
in bacteriology. The incident today cinched it. I asked a
stupid question about the type of media used to culture
tubercle bacilli and the other trainees and the mycologist
there gasped that I could possibly have gotten a degree
in microbiology without knowing that. And these last two
days have been a concentrated half-year course in medical
mycology, which of course is a review for everyone else.

Furthermore, I'm anxious to get our home set up and
you well on your way to the PhD. Then with things more
settled we can worry about more school for me. Actually, if
we stayed in California and if I continued in public health I
would almost have to go back for more courses.

March 12, 1961
I went down to Palo Alto yesterday and surprised my old
roomie and friend, especially my old roomie, who claims
that she's too busy to breathe, but I caught her sprawled
in her old study outfit on the floor playing solitaire. So
the poor girl had no excuse not to take two hours off from
her paper for lunch and a chat at St. Michael's Alley.
It's so refreshing and stimulating to breathe that college
atmosphere again. While at Guthrie, I rounded up a couple
of symphony tickets for March 29th. Don't you think that
this will be a good start on getting some of the cultural
activities of San Francisco before we move away?

6. Working in the Laboratory of a Nobel Prize Winner

In the letters in this chapter, Janey is suffering from impostor syndrome and doesn't truly believe she's qualified to win the job as a laboratory technician for Austrian-born Australian research biologist Dr. Gustav Nossal in his unit of the medical school's Genetics Department at Stanford. The department has a new and youthful director, Dr. Josh Lederberg, who has just arrived at Stanford after receiving the Nobel Prize in physiology and medicine. Janey gushes over how this full-time position is the dream of her life and how wonderful Dr. Nossal is. She's afraid she won't win the position because Dr. Lederberg has the final say and will see that she got a C in her genetics course, and even worse, he became outraged when he caught her removing scientific journal articles that he kept in the private library of his office.

During the year that Janey worked in the genetics lab, Dr. Nossal and British immunologist Avrion Mitchison mentored her to develop self-confidence in conducting independent research. When the 1960 Nobel Prize in physiology and medicine was awarded to Frank Macfarlane Burnet and Peter Medawar, there was great shouting and cheering in the Nossal laboratory, as if Nossal and Mitchison had won. It was, however, because Nossal and Mitchison were protégés of the Nobel Prize winners.

June 4, 1960

I am now in the lab waiting for the bacteria to grow. They don't reproduce fast enough for impatient me. I am now a reader for a bacteriology course and get all of $1.75 an hour [$12.75 in 2021 dollars]. I was so thrilled that they asked me to help them. I had thought that I was such an insignificant member of the department, if a member at all. Also, there is a slight possibility that I may be working part-time as a lab technician for Dr. Nossal in the Genetics Department. There's one other person ahead of me for the job. I had an interview last Thursday, and Dr. Nossal is the most wonderful person, a brilliant scientist with the most charming personality and true humbleness. He's recently from the Eliza Hall Institute in Melbourne and is not a cohort with Dr. Lederberg, the Nobel Prize winner. This job just seems wonderful, for it will become a full-time position in June under a visiting professor, Dr. Mitchison from England. The work is just up my line. That is, the problems that they are working on fascinate me. I do hope that I can get it as the experience will be invaluable and I may sneak off to classes throughout the year. So in a way it will be like taking directed research units under a professor. The only problem is that Dr. Lederberg has the final say on the matter and wants to look at my transcript—and of all things I got a "C" in genetics. Furthermore, he found me in his office library last quarter when I was doing research on the clonal theory. He has the most wonderful collection of references, some not found anywhere else in the school. But unfortunately he's one of those "hoggy" persons who allow no one to check any materials from the library, not even his grad students, and actually it's university property, and he dislikes a lot of people cluttering up his sacred domain. The next day after he caught another one of my department members in his library Saturday night, he posted a sign on his door instructing the janitor to kick out any unauthorized personnel in the department office when the secretaries have left for the day. So I am sitting on pins and needles right now.

I have just been informed by Mary, who is typing Dr. Lederberg's paper on space genetics, that I would meet the qualifications for space travel—female, dark skin, under 5' 5", black hair with heavy hair follicles, and flat-chested. If I can't find a job after grad school, there's always that possibility.

April 9, 1960
I have been lying out in the sun for the afternoon, after spending the morning injecting the foot pads of rats for Dr. Nossal. Quite a messy job as those animals do horrible things when they get excited, as you well know. Boy, I had to really grit my teeth and pretend I didn't care. The experiment is a continuation of the one I used so much as a reference in the paper. Seeing and doing it is so different from reading about it. And it can be so tedious and laborious as well as so detached if one doesn't think about the theory or look for new things in the procedure. Dr. Nossal is such a great person and so patient. He is constantly teaching me the implications and the mechanisms of each step, and his mind works so fast, especially when it comes to the math part in making dilutions of the inoculum. Yesterday when I was pipetting I forgot or didn't notice that the pipettes didn't have cotton plugs and so I swallowed a mouthful of live Salmonellae. No ill effects, but I hope that the bacteria in my mouth didn't affect the outcome of the experiment.

April 23, 1960
I think I'm still a bit uneasy when working with those mice and rats. I have to grit my teeth so hard, trying to be calm and not squeamish. I've gotten a bit better as time

110

progresses with not being so scared of their tails and bites, but I am still rather squeamish when it comes to their feces. I don't dare show it in the lab and sneak out to the "little girls' room" to wash my hands 101 times. Yesterday was my most spastic day and when carting the cages full of animals from the animal room to the lab, I overturned an entire case full of animals. So I spent most of the time chasing rats around in the room and mopping up broken water bottles and spilt saw dust. I would have thrown my hands up in desperation if Dr. Nossal weren't such a wonderful person. One just enjoys doing anything for him, even injecting rats.

You'll never believe that rats really do fly! I had a terrible time trying to get this particular rat into the jar as I am always afraid of giving an overdose of ether and then having to apply artificial respiration and oxygen. Anyway, this rat was giving me a pretty bad time—its reaction was so much faster than my slamming the cover over it. Well, it crawled on top of the cover and as I attempted to invert it, the brilliant little animal stood up and flew right into me. You should have heard the resultant piercing scream that shook the lab. Glad that you are working on a similar type of project and may understand some of the situations that often arise.

April 28, 1960

I have been getting the impression from Dr. Nossal that I can work in his department when I graduate as he went so far as to mention a raise in salary from the $1.50 to more when I go full-time. It's gotten so that I really love working there and would hate to leave it just as I am beginning to discover all the things that are going on.

This morning that lab was simply one joke after another. Gus (Dr. Nossal insists on me calling him by his first name these days, although I just can't quite condition myself to such informalities) and Ollie, a Dr. from Norway (whom I mistook for a lab tech when I first started there) were in their prime states, getting in on the excitement of the DeGaulle visit. Anyway, Gus thought that Josh Lederberg would be the perfect man as the standard bearer in the drum and fife welcoming band, waddling and rolling.

May 10,1960

I'm so impressed that you can inject rats all by yourself. I thought I would try today to see how it works. It doesn't. I was utterly panicked when Ollie asked me to inject some rats and then left me to my own contrivances. I was never so pleased to see Al, who also works part-time, come sauntering in.

June 4, 1960

Right now I'm so excited about working full-time. Gus is so amazingly kind and considerate. I still can't believe that I will sort of hold up production until I feel I'm ready to start. However, I think I will go in about once or twice a week to inject the rats as that has sort of been assigned to me and look over the mice colony. Those mice are worse than rabbits. We never seem to be able to keep pace with their reproduction rate.

June 25, 1960

The entire Biology Department and medical school and Microbiology Department were in a high state of excitement this week. The eminent Australian Sir

MacFarlane Burnet came to visit and give a series of
lectures. Gus was in a complete frenzy as he was Sir
Mac's former student and therefore in the role of Genetics
Department host. I hope you have heard of Sir Mac. His
name is practically godly in the fields of virology and
immunogenetics.

June 28, 1960
I was late for my first day of work. I dashed breathlessly
to the lab only to find it transformed into a nursery for
Gus's two darling towheaded children. Then I got some
instructions from Gus and plunged into work. But not too
successful work-wise—everything I laid hands on seemed
to take approximately ten times longer than it ever does
for Martha. After spending an hour setting up a titration,
I discovered the bugs used were no longer any good. They
had died of old age.

Something of interest: vol. LXXV #26 *Time* magazine,
page 53. Anyway I was impressed.[17]

July 3, 1960
In the next few weeks the lab will be looking more like
a classroom that it was designed for. Mitchison and

---

17 Janey sent me a two-page article from the June 27, 1960 issue titled "Progress in
Transplants." An excerpt:

What is wanted is a drug or chemical that will switch off the rejection
reaction so that the body will accept the transplant but leaving other
antibody mechanisms unimpaired. . . . It is being pressed with unusual
vigor at Stanford University. Radiologist Henry Kaplan is experimenting
in animals with massive doses of cortisone-type steroids. . . . Across the
courtyard in Stanford's department of genetics other researchers are looking
for answers. . . . Dr. Gustav Nossal is exploring the fundamental question
of why nature evolved the rejection mechanism in the first place. Likeliest
explanation: as a protection against infections by viruses and bacteria.

Engel will bring up the total of eight persons, sometimes ten, and so each is finally assigned his own little work corner. I don't know how anyone will be able to breathe. Everyone just lives for the day we move down into the windowless basement where the facilities are so much more convenient.

July 7, 1960
Our lab has gotten simply riotous as well as so busy. However, no one seems to be able to understand English. We have a complete cross section from Australia, Finland, Scotland, the Bronx, New York, and the Midwest. I am beginning to believe that I'm the only one who can speak English. Dr. Mitchison, the immunologist, is from Scotland—a dear man, very charming but humble. He can't quite get use to the idea of an assistant and therefore is ever so grateful whenever I lend a helping hand. Watching him, Gus, and Ollie, I can't help but try to visualize what it would be like to be married to a dedicated scientist. Absolutely heavenly. But then there is Dr. Mitchison, who injects 250 mice a day.

July 12, 1960
After work we went to the department barbeque in honor of this Japanese postdoctoral fellow who is returning to his homeland. I was particularly pleased to be able to meet the rest of the Genetics Department, especially those in the microbiology end of it, as we on the second floor are rather divorced from the greater part of the department, i.e., the Lederbergs (thank goodness).

I felt so fortunate to be able to talk to all the people in a social situation. The personalities are all extremely varied but surprisingly, most could talk about topics other than their work.

July 14, 1960

The pace of the experiments in our place is unbelievable. I'm sure that if I spent the next month reading solidly I still would not catch up with all aspects of their projects. Despite what appears to be very sloppy lab techniques, Gus is actually a very meticulous experimenter. He's forever giving me helpful hints and precautionary measures on things I never even give a second thought to. Another exciting thing is that he is constantly theorizing, which of course adds much stimulation. Many times he has conferences with other workers and he's very good about including me. But then, as I'm a paid worker there is a certain amount of work that I'm expected to put out, so unlike the rest of the crew, I can't just drop everything and listen. Still, I love the place and so far enjoy even the most menial tasks as there's a feeling that I'm helping them and it's appreciated. Today they probably wished I hadn't come in.

July 15, 1960

I have arrived at the conclusion that it's silly to try to rush about the lab so much. I really don't get much more done and I guess that with precision and efficiency I come out much better in the long run. The real problem is perhaps too many bosses, and when I'm free no one needs help, but once someone wants something done it seems that all the other four also require some help.

July 20, 1960

Yesterday the subject of the antibody workshop came up.

It will be held in La Jolla in December and Gus thought it would be a good experience for our devoted labor if he could take the whole crew along, me (a measly tech assistant) included. Gosh, I was flattered.

July 25, 1960
Oh what a day today! The morning was absolutely casual. I went wandering around drinking coffee and reading *Fortune* while waiting for my antigen to be washed and spun down in the centrifuge. Then afternoon and the pressure bore down. Between 5:30 and 6:00 p.m. I injected about 50 rats. Oh, I was hurrying so and the mother rats were so nasty because I tampered with their little children.

July 26, 1960
It was such a wonderful pleasure getting my first paycheck today as a real working girl. I dashed down to the shopping center the very minute I received the check, cashed it, paid long overdue bills, and tried to find a present for Mom and Dad, but not a thing appealed.

July 28, 1960
I have gotten more less settled down in the catacombs. I anticipate quite a relaxed setup for myself. I will be spending half time in the Nossal lab with six others and then half time with Mitchison, who has a huge lab all to himself. I was beginning to feel sorry for him being in the midst of all the dust and no equipment yesterday, but he still proceeded as usual with his mice work. Then I eavesdropped on a conversation he had with Dr. Rick from either CIT or MIT, a most stimulating talk. He has been

going to the Pugwash conferences[18] with Russian scientists, and he has become an avid advocate of stimulating scientists out of their little isolated labs and bringing them to the realization of their more important political roles in the troubled world. He feels that the Soviet thing is a real threat and shouldn't be sloughed off lightly. As I was busy injecting mice, I didn't get all the ideas he proposed.

August 10, 1960

I'm getting more and more at ease with the job. My complaints are really only because of the lack of anything else to complain about. And today it occurred to me just what makes me so tired at the end of the day: it's walking and standing on the hard cement floor.

I hope when you are down you will get to meet the rest of the immune-genetics group. They are what makes the day so pleasant for me. They certainly have been treating me with great tender loving care. Every day something hysterically funny comes up. Those foreigners do have a dry sense of humor.

August 11, 1960

Golly did I find it discouraging at work today. Things were getting a tad bit routine and the mice were biting so that I felt as if my fingers had gone through a meat grinder and were dripping with blood. It got to a point where killing mice, sucking up their blood, and grinding up their spleens was the most distasteful task ever. And then Dr. Mitchison's mice kept visiting other cages and escaping from their home and had to be ear clipped. For me, that ear

---

18 The Pugwash Conferences on Science and World Affairs, founded in 1957 to reduce the risk of nuclear and other weapons of mass destruction and first held in Pugwash, Nova Scotia. The organization still exists today.

clipping is an impossible chore. I had to resort to asking one of the animal keepers who had come down to visit to help me. Finally Mitch came upon the scene and sensing my distress, took over and sent me off making solutions, a task which he dislikes even more. But that was OK for me. However, I was so embarrassed when freshman chemistry slipped and I couldn't remember what a mole solution was.

When we got home Mary mentioned that she had to reread Dr. Mitch's manuscript. I took it up and was absolutely enthralled and thrilled. Seeing him discuss the problems that he wants to solve and his own data suddenly made me feel that my menial chores were not in vain, and that stuff is terribly fascinating. It's when one spends days upon days injecting mice that one simply does not give notice or even think about theories, and of course I don't have the capacity to begin to think about things. But with a definite statement like a manuscript the work seems significant, and what's more, I do have a share in it.

Guess what! My name will be appearing in print in some obscure thing like the *Australian Journal of Experimental Biology*. But nevertheless, it's going in print. Mary is typing up Gus's latest paper and she told me that I was acknowledged for invaluable technical assistance. So dear of him as it wasn't until recently that I began to help him and these immunology projects just take ages before results begin to show—12 months.

I enjoyed looking over the biology curriculum you sent. It certainly sounds as if some terribly exciting work is being done up there. Hmm, by no means a small place at all. I had been under the impression that the department was concerned with more basic biology, but instead there's quite a lot being done in genetics and radiation.

August 17, 1960

I must return to work from lunch and try to rectify my mistakes. Today I will be counting radiative antibodies in a huge complicated machine. But when transferring sera today I got the whole work so confused that I had to start over again. But then I hadn't enough blood, so I don't quite know what to do.

My "office" is the counting chamber down in radiology. Today's task consists of watching the little red lights go around and taking out a test tube containing tagged iodine precipitate after its rate of emission has been detected. What we have been doing is trying to paralyze the immune mechanism of mice against a given type of protein by giving them an overwhelming dose of the same stuff. As we will be looking for minute amounts of antibody this new Farr method was selected over the older classical methods that are read visually.

Monday we had our discussion session with the head of the medical school, who presented his data on the antibody action in patients with lupus erythematosus. What I am trying to say again is that it is these events that make my end of the research lab exciting. I admire and marvel at people like you who conceptualize all the tasks we perform.

August 30, 1960

Oh Richard, the most exciting thing of the day. I went back to lab after dinner to read some titration results. Ollie was there cleaning up some minute experiments before leaving for a conference in Japan tomorrow. He's begun to take a great interest in explaining the rationale behind the experiments to me. So inevitably we got to discussing the negative results of the last preliminary experiment.

Per usual I listened and nodded as if understanding and in agreement. Then I asked why it could not be done another way—hooking human "B" substance onto a mouse red cell and injecting it into mice, thereby initiating a higher antibody response. "B" substance, being a polysaccharide, is not strongly antigenic in itself. Oh, Ollie jumped as if I had hit on something spectacular. It seems that the only person who has used a similar system is Levine of the Landsstein group. He immediately invited me up to his house to discuss this possible experiment further with Dr. Mitchison, who was visiting there. We of course spent most of the time chatting as the women were there. Anyway, I suddenly felt like a pauper who had just inherited a million dollars. The thought of being included in a discussion with the bigwigs of the department is almost beyond comprehension, and to be treated more like a colleague instead of just a girl who injects mice.

It was really quite a scene. Three doctors—Ollie's wife is also an M.D.—sitting on floor of the old, old cottage, eating peaches and using a trunk for a coffee table, a sick little boy crying in the next room, the Mitchisons' little boys asleep in their homemade portable cradles, and Helen Makela pouring tea from a sauce pan as if she were at Buckingham Palace. You know, Richard, one can be so happy and lead a comfortable life, entertaining sincere good friends even without luxuries and modern gadgets. I'm so happy being with these people for a most pleasant evening, especially since they all have a wonderful sense of humor and good outlook on life as well as being dedicated scientists.

September 1, 1960

Gosh, with Gus, Ollie, and Al off on their trips the lab has
been delightfully quiet, and with Dr. Mitch coming very
late in the morning it's entirely peaceful with just us three
girl lab techs. I am certainly glad for a chance to straighten
up the lab and put things away (i.e., hide them so that they
wouldn't be able to find a thing when they return). I spent
an hour this morning chasing around the medical school
for a blood journal called *Vox Sanguine*—I'm attempting
to begin reading the literature before the lab hustles and
bustles again.

September 1, 1960

It was a very good feeling this morning when I walked
into the library and began looking up references again.
So much like a mole coming out into light after years of
hibernation. I'm very fortunate that Dr. Mitchison and
Ollie are so pleased that I'm doing something on my very
own. Dr. Mitchison today even offered his services to help
me get started on the experiment, even so far as helping
me pick out the mice to use. I will try to finish the article
tonight, but it seems to be taking me forever to finish but a
few short pages. I only hope that it will not prove too much
for me to handle. Come to think of it, I never before devised
my own experiment. I need your moral support even
though you don't know who Landerstein is.

September 7, 1960

Dr. Mitch was so sweet and concerned about my
experiment. I'm still looking up references and afraid to
start. I feel so ashamed when each day he asks how it's
coming along. But I'm afraid I'm not the go-getter.

121

The very day he arrived from Scotland, even before he found a place to live, he came to the lab and started making a protein to inject into mice. Poor Gus was trying to rush him so as to get him to the bank before it closed for some money to get him through the weekend. But his mice were more important and the bank had to wait.

Anyway, today Dr. Mitch felt I needed some human blood, so he had me type his blood and after discovering the type he dashed to the next lab and came back with a couple of cc's of his English blue blood.

October 7, 1960

I can't begin to tell you how delightful the party was this evening. Mary and I were probably the only outsiders among the eminent biologists. I learned from L. H. how to be the wife of biologist while he is still in school. I told them of the type of work you are doing and especially how you have to do everything yourself, i.e., making hamster cages, etc. Then her husband joined in and agreed that having to learn to do things by yourself and starting from scratch is one of the most invaluable pieces of experience you can get. And he also is in accord with you concerning the knowledge of every mechanism of your x-ray machine. As he says, you can't ever depend on having the knowledgeable technical staff to assist you, but you can better understand your data when you understand the mechanisms of the machine you use. And when little things go wrong, it is simpler to fix it yourself and impractical to have to wait for technical advice. What he meant was that the best way to understand the data produced by a device is to build the device yourself.

October 7, 1960

Everything possible that could go wrong in the lab did go wrong today. When I think of it I can't help but laugh. I couldn't use the warm room today so I had to bleed the rats warmed in the small incubator by myself. Oh, I've never had such fights in my life. I couldn't get them in the bleeding contraption and each time they moved I would lose my grasp and their tails bloody and all would go flying through the room. When Dr. Mitch came in to offer a hand, I felt a great gift from heaven. Just as we got started, Len came in with Tarasaki, whom Mitch had been waiting for all day. At the time he was holding a rat for me and in the most awkward position while I, nearly kneeling, attempted to get the silly tail in a 3 ml test tube and catch the dripping blood. Dear Dr. Mitch in the meanwhile looked as if he didn't know whether to simply greet Tarasaki and leave him standing there or shake his hand holding the rat but he decided to go calmly on with his work as if there had been no interruption.

Dr. Mitchison was at his usual prime today. By late evening his wine punch, served in a 6-liter beaker by others, had turned a much darker chianti red. Said he, "Just a change in pH." As we were leaving we commented to him about how his little boy was sleeping so peacefully amidst all the gaiety. We asked him how he managed it and he smiled very diabolically and slyly pointed to his glass of punch spiked with red wine. I so want you to meet these very casual, unaffected people, yet so friendly and gracious. Mrs. Mitchison was for the first time out of her flannel shirt and blue jeans and looking like Scottish nobility.

October 19, 1960

Mary was so wonderful today. She had taken one look at my experiment report and decided that it simply could not be turned in, so she spent two hours after work retyping everything.

October 20, 1960

You should have seen the people in our lab gloating this morning when they heard the names of the Nobel Prize winners: Burnet and Mewdawar! Gus is of course Burnet's protégé while Mitchison came from the Medawar school. From the way they were acting, it was if they themselves had won the prize. Well, tolerance and antibody production certainly have their place in the scientific world. And I'm very excited that I'm working so closely with their problems, especially that the outside world considers the projects significant and not so far out.

October 20, 1960

I spent the afternoon trying out my experiment. I think I've finally got it. I hooked a polysaccharide onto a mouse red blood cell. Now to inject it into the mouse and see if he will produce antibodies against the polysaccharide. My results were completely positive but the threshold difference in the test for reaction is so small that any result toward the positive is a good indication. I was especially pleased that the cells stayed intact after so much handling and about eight washings plus incubation with other materials. I am just thrilled to be able to do something entirely on my own. Of course, sweet Ollie was very interested in how I was progressing and even dashed up to the library to get some references that might offer some technical advice.

October 26, 1960

I'm very pleased to hear that you approve of taking the
Mitchisons and the Makelas to dinner. I guarantee that
you will find them socially delightful. They are very kind
and casual. Don't be shocked if Mitchison, the world-
renowned home graft expert, shows up at Ming's in his
plaid flannel rubber-soled shoes.

October 31, 1960

Dr. Mitchison is the true scientist, interested in his work
for the sake of pure valid experiments without thoughts of
prestige, etc. To him his experiment comes before anything
else. Nothing would stop him when is in the middle of an
experiment. He doesn't ask or try for prestige; he simply
goes about in his merry little way working on experiments
with nearly every imaginable person in the medical school
and even up in Berkeley. His following is unbelievable—it's
as if he were the Pied Piper.

When Mary mentioned to him about how secretaries at
lunch would compare the number of reprint requests their
bosses get (the sign of prestige, you know) he said that it
would be more impressive if his secretary told the girls
that she threw away 20 requests that morning. To him
reprints are silly—if people are that much interested in his
work, they can look it up in the library.

November 2, 1960

As you review biochemistry I think you may find this
experience noteworthy. While I was scurrying about in
the lab this morning with a handful of mice, a shy, gaunt
little British-looking man peered nervously in. I thought he
was just making a tour of the medical school as many nosy

people do, so I went about very preoccupied with my task. Later as I started to page Mitchison via phone, he walked in with Dr. M. and I proceeded to plague Dr. M. with 1001 questions that I had lined up (being that it's so hard to finally corner him). After I finished my questions, Dr. M. turned and said, "Excuse me, but I forgot to introduce you to a friend of mine, Jim Watson." He then suggested to his wife in blue jeans and Timothy, who had been waiting patiently, that they might take off a few minutes to take his friend to Kirk's for a Kirk burger. Later in the day I found out that the "friend" was none other than THE Watson of Watson–Crick DNA fame. As you can guess, I'm easily impressed.

It's a situation that's hard to solve[19] without leaving anyone stranded midstream. I agree with you on all the points you made. Only my devotion to Gus and his lab is very much like your devotion to Dr. Soderwall. He gave me my break when Lederberg was dubious about my application and he took great patience in training me. Perhaps there is a way in which I work a partial day, i.e., six to seven hours instead of eight. Then I can commute, which isn't bad via train. Secondly, I will have to think about a roommate until March.

I'm not trying to convince you that I should stay down here, which I don't really want to do and in fact really had planned to go back to San Francisco in January a few months ago. I just want to present some of the complications that are involved in my situation here.

What I am proposing is that I continue working for Gus and start commuting from San Francisco in January.

---

19 Janey is concerned that if she leaves the labs to begin her public health microbiologist training it will delay the completion of the research she is working on.

If it is too much of a strain, I can then look for something in San Francisco. It isn't too much to ask for a chance to experiment, is it?

November 6, 1960

This morning we talked over my job situation after I presented your "hourly" argument and they agreed that I should start looking for a job in San Francisco. So I will talk to Gus at the earliest convenient time and then check the situation at the University of California medical school. You are absolutely right about all the wasted time of catching trains and buses, etc.

November 7, 1960

How can I possibly live without you? To think out in detail and with deliberation all my problems. That was really a beautiful argument you plotted out. You now have the wholehearted, 100% support of the Young family. My leaving in January will be the only possible answer.

Last Friday Dr. Mitch had some visitors from the University of Edinburgh (his students) whom he had wanted to take to Chinatown for dinner, so naturally, he asked me for suggestions. I included in a very meagre list of suggestions the place of my personal interest, Kan's. So instead of working that afternoon I planned a menu, made reservations, etc. After I did that I really began to worry as those people at Kan's are such great snobs and one can never know how they would react to plaid flannel slippers. So after dinner in Chinatown Friday, Dad and I dashed up to Kan's to give the people sufficient warning and make sure that my boss would get the kingly treatment. It must have turned out all right, as both Av and Lorna beamed with grateful thanks today.

127

November 8, 1960

I heard from Ollie today. He's absolutely delighted to
join us for dinner during the Thanksgiving holidays.
However, there is another problem. What about Gus? I
personally wouldn't enjoy the casualness and friendliness
of the evening without him, as he seems more the type
who is more socially sophisticated and more conscious
of it. Perhaps it's just my own desire to be able to talk to
Av, Ollie, and their wives in a personal atmosphere. Just
an addition of two extra people makes it more difficult to
entertain. But again, it is really Gus whom I'm working for
and he's the type who would consider it more an affront if
he's not included when the other two colleagues in his lab
are invited. So maybe it is wisest to extend the invitation
and hope they will be busy that evening, since they usually
have quite a full social calendar.

The very saddest situation has struck. Our rat colony
has contracted pneumonia and they're dying off like those
rats in Camus' *La Peste*. Also, this bug has been incubating
and acting for a month or more so eventually apparently
healthy rats have already been exposed. Furthermore,
Ollie will be leaving in January, so there is no time left to
start new experiments.

November 10, 1960

While driving home today I realized I had completely
forgotten about an experiment that required injections
last Tuesday. I worried so about it all through dinner
that I went back to the lab. By some quirk of fate, Ollie,
who this experiment was for, came in and was even
forgiving enough to help me with the injections without me

requesting it. He was in a talkative mood and told me all about techniques of chromosome mapping. So I gained a lesson in genetics.

November 14, 1960

Gus was very understanding when I sprung the news on him. But I did promise to come in a few days in January if they happen to be swamped. That's the time when Ollie leaves and there's a slight chance that they'll be rushed then. However, from the looks of things they wouldn't be. I'm anticipating a very quiet week now and until December.

November 16, 1960

Today was one of the few days that Dr. Mitchison wasn't dashing all over the medical school and in fact spent most of the day in the lab. We talked about things in general and what I planned to do when I left. I was so complimented when he said it would be so hard for him back in Scotland without me around. And he went on to say that it would be a loss if I left this type of work. But truly, I don't want to be only a lab tech for the rest of my days.

November 20, 1960

I saw the Stanford bonfire rally (before the traditional game with UC) in action for the first time in my life. I had to ride home with Dr. Mitchison and family as Friday's rally ran late. But he and his wife wanted to stop by the lake[20] first, so crying babies were bundled in piles of blankets and all of us climbed the embankment in back of Roble Hall and stood in awe over the cheering crowds and

---

20 Lake Lagunita, an artificial dry lake on campus where football rallies are held. It was created in the 1870s to provide irrigation for Governor Stanford's Palo Alto stock farm.

gaily playing band. A beautiful sight. I so wished we had been in love while in school and during Big Game.[21]

December 1, 1960

Your "cloud" card was just the shot I needed tonight. Absolutely tired and grouchy after work tonite. The boredom of the titrations was simply unbearable. The same routine for the past few weeks has made a robot out of me. Sweet Av, just back from Los Angeles, was very consoling because he was ever so apologetic in his shy boyish manner for subjecting me to such a task. However, because it was getting me down, I made a point to finish off every last serum (about 150) this afternoon for about a month. It also means that I've worked myself out of a job for a while. Now I will have to play mathematician for a few weeks, calculating the results.

A bit of irony—Gus came back completely haggard after discussing the budget with Joshua. It seems we are economically in bad straits. We have spent $8,000 over the grant and have only $2,400 left for supplies for the next six months [$72,000 and $21,600 in 2021 dollars]. So we got the word to slow up on orders for things we don't absolutely need or else think twice before buying. We then went into a long discussion of financial problems of scientists. Josh feels that oftentimes inferior scientists get large grants and can attract better technicians, students, etc., whereas better men, i.e., biologists at Stanford, use bailing wire. Len, who has been trained to work within tight budgets, feels that better scientists come out of being forced to use their own ingenuity and making the most of what

---

21 I was a member of the Stanford marching band.

they have. As you can probably guess, Gus is of the other opinion and said he doesn't worry about such things but will leave the financial problems up to Josh. Gus is getting irritated with Josh for not getting to his paper submitted since September so is perhaps retaliating.

While leaving work today, I was doing some self-pitying about how routine my workday is. Then I saw E. sitting in the dark under the rain waiting for the bus. I realized how lucky I am to have you, working with wonderful people, and really variety in work compared to her day of dishwashing at the lab.

December 5, 1960

Our conversation concerning my being with you when you're studying reminded me of a comment made by Joshua Lederberg. He said that L. H. would be a great scientist if he weren't so biologically inclined toward his wife (she was the woman who came into Av's lab to use the centrifuge and remarked that she had seen you around before.) Do you think I should limit the time that I'm with you?

December 6, 1960

I had the shock of my life when I got to work yesterday and discovered that there are about two weeks of titration left to be done. This time we're testing the avidity of antibody and instead of 3 tubes per sera there are 20 tubes. J. came out of Gus's lab to do a set and AV realized how "wretched" those tubes are, in his own words. Anyway, it's all very discouraging that titration of one sort or another never ends in immunological work.

7. Training to Become a Public Health Microbiologist

After graduating from Stanford, Janey had three options: continue working at Stanford, which would require commuting from San Francisco, get a lab technician job in San Francisco, or enter the California state public health microbiologist certification program. She chose the latter.

January 5, 1961

The working atmosphere and people [in the California state public health lab] are most friendly. I feel as if I'm being waited on hand and foot and they're very patient with my bumbling lab techniques. It's only me who gets impatient with people who give exacting explanations repeatedly or tell me something that I consider common knowledge. In all it's a good training program with lots of time out for coffee in the morning and tea in the afternoon!! And the people aren't wastrels but in fact keep up with the literature at every spare moment. It's a healthy atmosphere.

On the bus today, I did a bit of calculation: 9 hours at work, 3 hours of commuting, and 8 hours of sleep left very few hours a day. Thanks to you, I gave up the idea of going down to Palo Alto every day. That really would have been a strain.

The training program is turning out to be quite an education, primarily a good review of microbiology, also in putting some of the facts that I was forced to memorize into practice. And on a slow day like today I had a chance to prowl through the journals and texts. They even have a journal closet.

What I don't like is the routine that controls the lab. There's a designated day, nearly to the hour for everything. People arrive promptly at 8:00, coffee exactly at 9:45, lunch at 12:00, tea at 3:00, and at 5:01 the Pubic Health building has not a single person in sight. Methods are standardized so meticulously that even liquids must be dropped into a bottle from a pipette a certain way. So different from my haphazard life in the Mitchison lab. I'm beginning to miss the easygoing atmosphere and being able to do things differently if it's more convenient. However, I think I do need a bit of regimentation, especially since I can't go fast or try to hurry here. Now you'll never have to hear about my working too hard.

January 8, 1961

Thank you for goodie #1. It now is stuck proudly on my public health training folder, which I just retrieved from the police department today (I left it there during the frenzy of having my car towed away). Goodie #2 looks very interesting, but never having come across most of those names before, I didn't understand what is to be covered—only genetics sounded familiar. You didn't know I was a pseudo biologist, did you?

January 11, 1960

Yesterday a couple of the girls in the lab went to hear a lecture and the lecturer was none other than Gus! So today I was in my glory explaining to the people who attended the lecture more of the details of single-cell technology. They were thoroughly impressed with Gus and his lecture, so you can imagine how wonderful I felt having worked with such a high-powered man. My supervisor is trying to

Janey Young on her wedding day, July 9, 1961

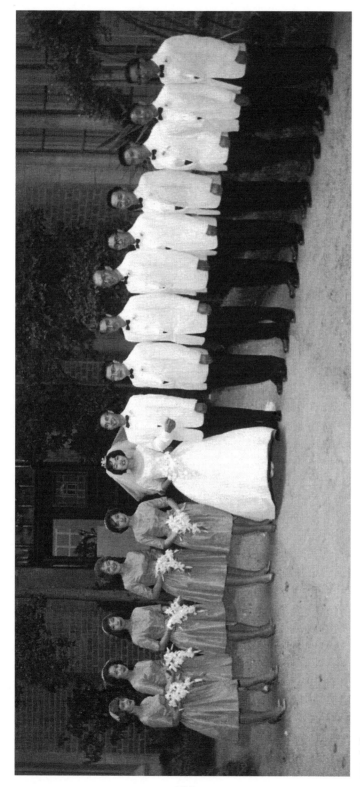

Wedding party

Janey's t-shirt: "I'M A BIG DEAL DMTS," 1982

Distinguished member of the Technical Staff Awards
(front row: left, Terry Alger; right: Janey Cheu)

Richard's ordination as a deacon, June 2003

50ᵗʰ wedding anniversary celebration, 2011

corner me into giving a talk in the monthly journal about antibody production. Actually I know much less than they do but having worked closely with the problem has certainly added to the prestige factor. However, on the technical side of things I'm not at all adept. Gosh, do I feel disorganized and all left hands. Pipetting with my mouth has been my greatest downfall. Fortunately the girls here are all very sweet and patient, never getting upset with all my mistakes.

Whew, what a hectic day. Nothing like that at Stanford, but I couldn't get any test to work. Quite frustrating when everything has to be minutely exact; e.g., while diluting the test antigen, I shook too hard like the bus is shaking now.

I have discovered many girls in the lab who manage both marriage and children and even husbands going to school. They seem to have survived well and stay beautiful, especially this one particular Chinese girl who's worked for years, has two little girls, and looks fresh out of college. The rest of the crew, however, is less fortunate—mostly old-maid career women. As a whole, they seem very different from the girls in Palo Alto. Probably the age difference.

January 12, 1961
The people at work certainly have a lot of different interests that keep them occupied in their off hours. Even on the job during lunch a group of them gather once a week to play the recorder. And there is one who is a gourmet cook, a good prospect for some recipes. I talked again with the Chinese girl and learned that the babysitter for her two girls costs only approximately $100 a month. And with her first child she worked until seven days before the baby

138

came because she didn't know when it was due. She took a month off and was back at work again.

January 15, 1961
The public health work really is not at all hard to adjust to, but it's simply me who is more restless than most people, hating to sit still. I used to react the same way down at Stanford, if not more strongly. Weeks upon weeks of injecting mice and rats, then weeks of bleeding them, then came the titrations. I will certainly keep in mind your good advice about accepting the work as it is and not try to compare. And I promise to not fight the job. Honestly, I do enjoy most of it, but like everything else, I can't bring myself to love every bit of it.

January 20, 1961
I have a test today and I'm as panicked as I used to be before taking finals at school. I didn't do a very good job of studying. I enjoyed reading more about theories and history than memorizing the technical procedures, so I fear that I may not do very well. A long, boring test, parts of it anyway. In two hours and after eight full pages I only completed half of two sections. I'm pleased that it's not graded as I was terribly verbose and repetitious.

I'm truly beginning to enjoy the ride home. It's a thrill each day crossing the bridge at sunset. The colors are all at once vibrant and serene. It changes each day so it's always interesting. I would be so pleased if your dad could paint it for us so we could have a moment of it captured forever. It's very much the same as watching antigen dry up on a slide and seeing crystals form under dark-field illumination. This was shown to me by a girl who plays the recorder, cooks exotically, and weaves her materials. A character of course and I really enjoy seeing her in action!!

January 23, 1961

I was in a new section today learning to do Kalmer's modification of the Wasserman syphilis test. I followed the main technician around like a faithful dog, just watching and getting more bored because I couldn't do any actual work.

February 1, 1961

I'm gradually beginning to feel that my background experience is mounting. The decision to take this training program, I think, is probably the wisest that I could have made. In this short month I've probably learned more than in the six months at Stanford. That is, what I learned at Stanford was in a way limited to my background and most seminars were somewhat above me. And the work didn't prepare me for much outside of injecting mice and rats. From a mercenary standpoint, I doubt if I can make more anywhere else. If I continue at California Public Health my yearly salary will approach $5,500 [$49,500 in 2021 dollars] or greater depending on what local department I will work for. It really is a good feeling to know that I can make use of my education in this way. And I hope that the broader education will help me become a good wife for you.

Most of the day was devoted to learning about the Rh blood group system. Then at 4:00 we stopped for a lecture given by a girl who has just completed a course in immune chemistry. For me it was exciting to build my particular knowledge of immunology further. Now I wish I had taken notes at seminars at Stanford as there was a great deal of reference to some of the work there and I couldn't remember much of what I had heard formerly.

February 3, 1961

This lab is different from most clinical labs or local labs where the quantity of work keeps one occupied the entire day. It's more a reference lab and allows time to work on new procedures and techniques. I derive the greatest enjoyment throughout the day when I can thumb through books and reprints. So as a result I got quite a bit of reading done. I was taken aback when one of the trainers told me that as a trainee I didn't have to know the material I was reading and suggested a condensed version.

February 7, 1961

This week at the lab I've been given ten evaluation specimens and am left to my own. So I've been bumbling along. I am enjoying working alone without having people breathing down my neck. And I have more time to think procedures through and suffer through poor planning and execution.

February 7, 1961

There's another Chinese girl who commutes to Berkeley on the F bus with me and today we started talking. That is, she initiated the conversation. It was very refreshing talking to a girl like her. She is only 19, but just eloped with one of those typical Chinatown hoods. I was impressed with her attitudes toward life and marriage. Her education and manner of speech are limited but it's her ideas and optimistic attitudes that are so beautiful. To her life is wonderful, yet she accepts disappointments.

What I mean is that she is happy with simplicity and doesn't envision what she doesn't have. My, she did chatter throughout the trip to and from work. I felt as if I know her life history and I am very attached to her friendliness and freshness. It's surprising the type of friends one can make on a bus. Another time I'll tell you about the woman on the Geary bus.

February 14, 1961
Fascinating afternoon at the radiation lab. It's their new setup and the equipment is overwhelming! They have about 20 of those counters that we had at Mitchison's lab plus one that cost $25,000 [$225,000 2021 dollars] which does about 120 different operations at once as well as remembering the radiation spectrum it picks up. After the tour I really feel a great respect for the California Public Health Department. It is a dynamic place with great emphasis on advancing and providing good health programs for people's safety—a good state to live in. The radiation department itself, in a way, serves as a check on the activities of the Atomic Energy Commission and also is working on mammals' intake of radiation in food, air, water, etc.

February 15, 1961
We are getting a concentrated course of analytical chemistry crammed into our little brains the last two days. The Food and Drug lab was today's mark. Oh, stories of how butchers adulterate meat and crooked pharmacists highlighted the usually pedantic lectures. Most of the work employs that great instrument, the recording spectrophotometer or chromatography techniques. To the

biologist (pseudo like me) this is all very mysterious but exciting.

February 23, 1961

The strain of mycology today was enough to shake the strongest person's nerve. Today I discovered why I feel so antagonistic toward the instructor. It reduces down to her hypertensive attitude. It's quick, quick, quick everything! She has to peer through everyone's scope at the same time. In spite of if all, we sponged up a pyramid of info on dermatophytes. Yep, we covered the entire group within six hours.

8. Janey's Encouragement of Her Future Husband's Career

My physician father wanted me and my brother to become medical doctors. I occasionally "shadowed him" on house calls at night when mom wanted me accompany him. I would sit in the car waiting for him. When he returned, he would describe the nature of the patient's problem. Once, he had me scrub up and observe a hysterectomy operation. It was technically interesting but didn't motivate me to pursue a medical career. I was interested in biology and becoming a professor, not a doctor. Fortunately, my brother entered medical school, which made Dad very happy and allowed me to pursue my academic interests.

In 1952, I was admitted to San Francisco's academic public high school, Lowell High School. The teachers taught at an academic level I had not experienced before. I decided I wanted to become a biologist and wished to learn more than was taught in the classroom. I asked the biology teacher, Miss Vasquez, if I could help her set up the labs after school was out. She agreed and I became the first biology laboratory assistant at Lowell. She taught me the principles of biological research and how to explore topics of interest, and instilled a discipline for careful note taking in me.

During my freshman year at Stanford, my interest in biology was further stimulated by a course taught by the department chairman. I spoke to him so often after class that he gave me a tiny space in the Biology Department basement—a closet under a staircase—to conduct independent research, without any oversight from a professor, and permission to draw supplies from the supply room. I studied the anatomy of a species of lizard found on campus. When I attended UC Berkeley as a sophomore and was at home caring for my dad after my mom's death, I did independent research on the pituitary gland in the head of bullfrogs. One day, one of my decapitated frogs reflexively jumped off the laboratory table and hopped way, and I had to chase it down the hallway past amused faculty and students.

During my junior year at Stanford, I was a laboratory assistant to Dr. Page, the senior botanist on the biology faculty. I took a course on embryology taught by Dr. Clifford Grobstein[22] and instantly became infatuated with embryology. I shared my enthusiasm with him. In my senior year, he appointed me an undergraduate research fellow and provided me with laboratory space to do independent research. I was treated as a graduate student and attended seminars and presentations with the other graduate students.

In 1959, I learned of the U.S.A.F.'s efforts to put a human in space and that it was conducting animal experiments at Holloman Air Force Base in New Mexico. I wrote a letter to the program and asked to be a biology intern in the summer of 1959 after graduating from Stanford. To my amazement, I was accepted and was the only biology intern on base. Everyone else was an engineer. The Russians launched the Sputnik satellite into space in 1957 and the United States was afraid that the Russians would rain down atomic bombs on us at will. The internship introduced me to applied research and I assisted the chief veterinarian. After my summer internship, the lab named one of the chimpanzees "Chew," which was reported in the *San Francisco Chronicle*.

During my final year at the University of Oregon, I was trying to decide on a career path in biology. Janey followed each step with great interest, as reflected in her letters. She was excited about the opportunities available to me. Equally important, my progress encouraged her to believe that she could also have a career in science.

---

22 Dr. Grobstein's obituary in the *New York Times* on September 13, 1998, read, "Dr. Grobstein made important contributions to the study of cancer and of developmental biology. But he was widely respected by fellow scientists for his ability to analyze the human implications of medical research and technology. He became dean of the newly formed school of medicine at San Diego which under his leadership became a highly regarded teaching and research institution."

December 1, 1960

I'm glad to hear that the Tuesday noon discussions
are progressing. A brilliant idea on your part and it's
big, efficient planning (good equilibrium between inner
direction and building brotherly concerns with fellow
students).

I am most excited about Dr. Sody's recommendation.
Having a fellowship will be the very best possible situation,
primarily if it doesn't limit you and require that you put in
so many hours of outside work per week.

But still I hope you'll continue to talk to other people
and look in on other setups. Not that I don't like Oregon,
but I do want you to have a wide experience and know
more about what others are doing in fields you are
interested in.

December 6, 1960

I'm pleased Sody has released you during the holidays. I
promise that you'll get some studying done . . . not all the
time, though.

December 11, 1960

I am so sorry that you were disappointed in Sody's lecture.
But don't feel that your idol's shining armor has tarnished
or begrudge him for his lack of initiative and fiery pursuits.
For you, he was indeed a gift from heaven because through
his kindness you found your way in science and research.
Only now you've outgrown what you can learn from him
academically but never his friendship and guidance. The
above lines probably sound utterly trite and pedantic as I
know you would never brush Sody off like so many others
in the department.

Last Friday night you sounded so disillusioned and I feared that you were ashamed that you had placed so much confidence in this man who lost this particular race—the seminar—and therefore you want to sever your trust and allegiance. While you are with him, put out your very best work for him. Professors grow with their students too!

January 7, 1961
You sound enthusiastic about your new job. I'm so thrilled that you are enjoying it so much. What a wonderful opportunity to get an inkling of what is ahead for you in your career. And you do seem more relaxed mentally, not in the sense that you're not thinking, but being freed from the mental anguish.

January 8, 1961
I'm of the opinion that you sent me on a wild goose chase, but it was an enjoyable one. The binder was easy enough to locate, the letters and applications were there as you said (I'd never imagined anyone being so neat and organized in keeping records), but I don't think that the record was filed with the rest. With your dad looking also, we found your letter to the Testing Service asking for the application for the GRE to be given on January 16, 1958, but was that the same as the one whose results you were so gleeful over in spring quarter 1959? Also among the papers was mention of your taking the medical school admission test on May 3, 1959.

I agree with your trying to verify a scientific fact and approve of your standing by your belief. The problem is very subtle, however, and that is in how your case is brought out and proved. One has to be shrewd in showing someone that he is wrong. One almost needs political finesse for this, for the lecturer may think that a high-hatted student wants to show him up and fellow students may also be under the impression that you are trying to snow your professor. It's tricky business and should be handled with discretion.

January 15, 1961

I'm so excited about your new teaching position! Don't you feel on top of the world having a section of your own? I can imagine it must be a double pleasure not having to share the class. But are you sure this will leave enough time for your studies and not develop any pressures? It's also encouraging to have a man like department chair Tepler fighting for you. It's a very good indication of how the department feels toward you.

January 18, 1961

I do wish I were up there with you when you are applying to various schools. It is exciting for me to look through other school catalogues and see how the academic world operates in various parts of the U.S. Are you by chance still planning to investigate the possibility of Florida? I gather that your influence at Illinois is rather impressive, with both Sody and Licton on your side.

January 23, 1961

I am very proud that you are so devoted and interested in your students to give them special review sections, etc. I regret I didn't have you as a teacher. On the subject of learning, the newsreel last Saturday included pictures of your chimps at the airbase playing pattern games. What delightful actors they are on the screen. The audience was in an uproar. Now which one of them was named Chew?

January 24, 1961
I do approve of your feelings of obligation to your students; in fact as I mentioned before, I am pleased that you enjoy teaching as much as you do. My fear was that you might be selling yourself short on time as you so far haven't made any mention about reviewing for March, but I see that you are getting a review this way. As you worried about my devotion to the work in Palo Alto, I too am concerned that you might be working under too much stress and strain. In spite of it all, I'm pleased that you are so much happier this quarter.

January 25, 1961
Your letter was most thrilling! Your friend Dr. Steggerda sounds delightful, down to earth yet dynamic in his work as well as with people. I wholeheartedly (from what I've read in the experiment) believe that he is a good prospective teacher. Nevertheless, I can't help but get the feeling that a grad student at Illinois is left very much on his own, remembering also that the student-professor ratio at Illinois is rather high. I would dread seeing you in the same situation that you are now in with Sody, who allows your independence but in no way guides or leads. I guess the one statement that disturbs me is, "A lot of times our advising could be nothing more than a representative of the grad staff who is available to help when necessary."

But if you were interested in Steggerda's work enough to work closely with him to obtain a good start in research, it would be more beneficial for you than charging right into the school and doing creative work, which appears to be the attitude of the school. Last word on Steggerda's letter: I am thoroughly impressed with its friendliness, personal tone, and abundance of information with a few sentences. But that comment on "H of a place to spend Xmas"— was that his statement or your own personal stamp of approval?

January 26, 1961

Very excited to know that you've gotten to the section of biology to be covered in the orals. Perhaps I simply panic at the word "test," but oral just horrifies me! However, I must make a pact with you: I'll do all the worrying and you will do the studying but we'll pray together. Okay? I am very glad to know your enthusiasm about Steggerda's work. It's also particularly useful that you know one of his former students. And no doubt Sody can give you an honest opinion as well as some more insight on the man you haven't met.

January 31, 1961

Hearing of your PhD school application plans is progressively becoming more and more thrilling. People all over seem to like and want you, so I can't help but gloat and feel warm, filled with pride.

February 1, 1961

How could you begin to compare my hectic days with yours when you start at 4:00 a.m.? You certainly accomplished a whirlwind storm Tuesday. And I can see that you are definitely getting more and more out of your visits to different departments. What's new, this red carpet service is most indicative, isn't it? I can visualize that your decision in April will be a difficult one to make.

February 13, 1961
You should be able to get into any school with a recommendation such as that from Sody to Yates! The differences in those two letters are so great that one won't have believed that they were about the same person.

February 28, 1961
Mission accomplished: I called your dad to give him the good news that you passed the French test.

March 7, 1961
It was so pleasant and wonderful to hear your strong, deep voice. And it was a great relief that you've made it through half of the ordeal of your final oral exam for your master's. We won't give Stanford another thought. Besides, we never gave it much thought in the first place. The most important thing for you is getting through the next week, and we can take things as they come.

March 9, 1961
Congratulations! I could barely control the phone receiver, much less the flow of tears. My master of arts in biology recipient. I'm so proud of you, I had to tell the world even though at the time it was just the small world of microbiology. They all had to know. And I am also so happy that you didn't balk at any of the questions they presented, even in statistics. Hmm, job very well done. I can well imagine that you must be feeling as limp as a rag doll after the release of all the tension and months of preparation.

But you must give yourself a huge celebration and then enjoy relaxing during your last seven days in the rain country. It's also the opening of a new world and a new vista for us.

March 12, 1961

Mrs. Wilbur has been informed by your private secretary of the great event, the results of all your tests. As you might have known, she was most pleased and wants you to be sure to give her a call when you get back.

Your celebration with Sody and the group must have been a sight to remember—the ultraconservatives drinking it up in the afternoon sun. Sody really needed his student to come through as you did to boost up his spirits and even restore some of his own confidence in himself.

9. We Didn't Tell Our Parents We Were Engaged

My relationship with Janey developed suddenly and intensely after that New Year's Eve date because we were separated by hundreds of miles and only saw each other on my very short visits to San Francisco during breaks in my school schedule at the University of Oregon. That meant that we were quite enthusiastic about each other when we did meet. When we were together, we were in our own small world in an orbit beyond Earth, intensely focused on being with each other. We didn't socialize with anyone else, especially our parents, who asked too many questions. When we decided to become engaged, we were so excited about having made the decision that we didn't think of sharing it with anyone else, including our parents, until after I had already returned to Oregon. Then reality set in and we had to figure out how to tell our parents and relatives.

July 11, 1960

I am more inclined to think that when we make that all-important announcement that it would be better to have more time for planning. And also, as much as I like surprises, I'm not sure how the surprise would affect our respective families. I have a feeling that concerning this special occasion, my parents are rather old-fashioned. I remember a couple of years back when my cousin George (my parents were his legal guardians as his dad died before his birth and his mother was in Hong Kong) called Mom the night he was going to surprise his fiancée with the ring and how very hurt and upset Mom became because she didn't even get to see the ring first. Of course this was his own personal affair, but his parents felt that they deserved some degree of respect by letting them know of his plans. Surprises are a funny thing—one never quite knows how the other party will react to it all. So I think that your first idea about the "personal" touch may be better in the long run. If you don't think that a weekend is too rushed, the latter part of August is really as good a time as any. That will give us 11 months. Do you approve of long engagements?

It still leaves me spellbound, but Dad takes such an interest in you as he has never done with any other of my male friends. He used to be so jealous and sullen that I would never dare invite a boy upstairs to greet the family, although Mother insists upon it simply because she's so nosy. The first thing Dad asked when he was driving me home to dinner was "How's your dear boy?" Then he told me that he saw your father and stepmother Alice at the Imperial Palace buffet lunch and all were so congenial. One would expect that they were anticipating something.

July 13, 1960
The more I think about it the more I like it: the 20th of August to announce our engagement, of course. And I'm sure that I've become just as anxious as you are, but it must be presented so that it wouldn't give our families heart failure. Actually, I have a slight notion they may be quite pleased—mine, that is—as far as I can gather.

July 14, 1960
Golly jeepers! In a few hours it will have been a month

154

since we got engaged, and by August 20th it will be over two months. Now do you think that we're being good children by hiding it from our parents? Just rationalizing. I have definitely made up my mind for the 20th, provided that it's agreeable with you.

July 15, 1960
Congrats: you are now a fiancé of one month. Rather incomprehensible, n'est-ce pas? The month certainly flew by and next year will probably be here before we get accustomed to the idea of our engagement. Oh, on that comment about long engagements, I guess I don't write English or something. It was made in reference to the time we should cue our friends and relatives of the situation. And practically, to set the all-important date any sooner would be too hectic, although emotionally, I'm ready at your beck and call.

July 20, 1960
Do you realize it's exactly one month before August 20th? Already I'm ever so excited and up in the air. I guess I'm worse than an eight-to-five secretary who spends the day watching the clock.

Of course I'm not mad that you told Jim. I wish we could in fact tell the entire world. Many times I barely can contain myself and nearly have let the secret out. And when they try to pry into our plans I revert back to going through your schooling schedule. Mother commented that by that time Dad would be too old to walk me down the aisle.

Oh, you should have seen Dad at the wedding of his friend's daughter on Sunday. Never has he concentrated so hard on every detail of the ceremony, down to counting the number of rows of seats in the church, and sort of smiling to himself. I didn't dare look at him in fear that I would laugh myself into hysterics.

The mention of John C. reminds me—he had his wedding ring and Annie's designed by Matt Kahn, the same person I took the design course from and for whom I have such great admiration, even though some people have described him as an "articulate little bastard." He's the same artist who did that "Cat under the Willow" picture that hangs over the bed in my apartment. I get sentimental whenever I see his work or hear his name as his course opened to me a new realm of insight and interest in art. Also he usually complimented many of the things I did. A kind word from him is nearly like hearing from God as he's usually so sarcastic and critical, making people feel like a fool most of the time. But I like him and an idea came into my mind for the design of my ring.

July 22, 1960
Richard, they just played a selection from *Pal Joey* on the radio, and I dreamt of you with me listening to it. I'm so glad you approve of Matt Kahn designing my engagement ring. It will be so wonderful and so personal. I'm ever so excited.

July 24, 1960
Finally since the summer began I had a good talk with my sister. You no doubt can guess the topic of discussion. We really covered the subjects well. It was so good that we are both in the same situation and can talk so freely as well as be good listeners. It must be amusing for a viewer to

sneak in on us two girls and see us laughing and crying intermittently every minute. But we still reminisced, discussed problems, and dreamt about the future. Guess what I discovered to be so amusing: John's not getting a ring either. She put it this way: "She doesn't want a thing to distract from his beautiful hands." Now why don't practical people like me think like that?

August 3, 1960

I don't know about your relatives, but on my side the news will fly like wildfire so I doubt if our personal message would be any faster. However, it would be the appropriate thing to at least pay one visit to my grandmothers. So brush up on your Chinese. I haven't met any of your relatives other than Aunt Paula, so I would love to meet the rest of the Cheu clan if we have time.[23]

You know, as you begin to make practical plans and suggestions, the prospect of the 16th of July for our wedding becomes more and more thrilling and wonderful and it doesn't seem as far off. I'm a dreamer and just need someone as practical as you are. I would be completely lost without you.

August 5, 1960

I was thinking it might be a good idea to cue your father in on your intentions before making the announcement. Honestly, I really worry about the effect it may have. Can you imagine all ten champagne glasses clashing to the floor simultaneously and then dead silence? Oh, I shudder. I'm much too chicken for too dramatic surprises. We might announce the date on the night of the 20th and surprise the

---

23 My Aunt Paula and Uncle Guy were my only relatives.

rest, but not your dad. It also occurred to me, do we have the right to announce things without my dad's permission? I haven't read up on Emily Post so I don't know.

August 15, 1960

Time necessitates a short quick letter—but then, even a long letter can't fully express my full beautiful day. Poor Don was detained slightly again at the hospital but we arrived at the Chesbro family wedding just as the procession started, so we had to stand in the foyer while they went in. Actually we had a better view and the participants didn't look as contrived as they usually shake and stumble down the aisle before the several hundred guests within the church proper. The setting was beautiful, a simple wooden Episcopal church decorated with delicate white flowers. Especially impressive were the white-robed candle bearers that preceded the bride and attendants. Then we were given permission to take seats in the church after all the bridal party had gone in, and by strange coincidence the next vacant seats were right next to your dad and Alice. Oh, your dad was most attentive, peering over shoulders so that not a detail was missed. However, as the ceremony got longer and longer he became a bit restless. As we came out, he said to me that it was longer than a Catholic ceremony. (Now aren't you glad I'm not Episcopalian?) The reception was held at the house of Uncle Wayne, a wonderful home in Berkeley. And of course, I met your delightful Chesbro grandparents. Your grandma is the most lovable person ever and I spent most of the time chatting with her. The rest of the family was as wonderful and so sweet to me. And Don and Lil took excellent care of me.

158

August 23, 1960

Connie, in precise detail complete with facial expressions
and hand motions, has demonstrated Al's and her visit to
your hamster lab. Her description of your intenseness and
calm was just too much for me to take. Also talked to my
mother this evening. She was very pleased that you called
before you took off. It was difficult to get going again in the
lab today after the heavenly weekend. The clouds are still
so high after announcing our engagement. The people in
the lab were so happy for us. They are indeed so dear.

August 29, 1960

How very devious of you to call your dad knowing full well
that I would be there. Excellent timing. Of course your dad
was very dear about it, and kidded me all evening about
you not really wanting to talk to him.

September 9, 1960

I ran a most important errand this afternoon, a visit
to Gleem's, the jeweler. I probably frustrated the poor
salesperson to no end, violating every rule in the jewelry
trade. But the ring designed for a smaller stone was
what I wanted. The larger mount I thought was much too
chunky and the holes on the side were incredibly silly.
Furthermore, I happen to like to wear rings loosely, not
quite as loose as the original, but loosely. However, the
lady insisted that such atrocities to rings are unheard of.
Being that I would be the sole wearer, I finally got my way.
They will have to send back to New York for the ring, but
with telegrams, air mail, etc. these days they should have
it here by Friday. It probably would be wise to have the
stone sent down to me so that even if they receive the ring

on Friday morning they could have the completed ring ready for you when you get to Palo Alto in the afternoon. Then too, you wouldn't have to worry about whether or not you have to be down here earlier. Oh, I'm absolutely excited about everything!

September 10, 1960
Although I first said that engagement rings are superfluous, I've changed my mind. I have to save situations such as the following. The boy I met at the Chinese Students Conference (last month) called and asked for a date. I had to tell the poor boy, who was already shaking, that I had a dear fiancé. I thought I had avoided dates with Chinese college men when I put a San Francisco address and phone number (rather than Stanford) on the address list they published of all the conferees, or I would leave the group when they started dancing or socializing. Yep, I want to wear your sign of possession. A pin is fine but most Chinese squares think, "What a pretty charm."

September 25, 1960
I can't help but spend at least half the day looking at my beautiful ring and waving it around so the whole world can see. It is a wonderful symbol of our love. Thank you.

September 26, 1960
Oh, I opened a letter meant for you. I thought it was very amusing that the mailman put a question mark on the envelope next to your name. It was the appraisal complete with the most beautiful ever photo. Oh, most impressive but most of all I enjoy wearing the original.

October 2, 1960

I like your idea of staying in San Francisco after the wedding. There is still so much of San Francisco that we haven't had a chance to enjoy during your very hasty trips. We still haven't gone to a symphony together, just one pop concert. Did you ever go to the San Francisco Symphony while at Stanford?[24] I did use to look for you whenever I noticed that Tigre had a box, just out of curiosity, being such a nosy person.

October 3, 1960

All today I tried to analyze my feelings and why I caused you so much frustration with my teasing. I concluded that most of the time, I, like the rest of the family, especially Mom, tease out of love. And then again, I remember how I used to torture boys with my teasing simply because I was backed into the corner and had to resort to this form of counterattack. Extremely naughty and I do hope I never use the latter on you. Basically, it's my inner fear of being on the defensive, so I revert first to the offensive before any forces have been mobilized. Please catch me whenever you feel that I'm playing horrid games, at least not over serious matters.

Mom, Dad, and my grandmother (not the one you antagonized) arrived completely loaded with groceries, pastries, and flowers to brighten up the place, but not as nice as the roses I received from you. It seems Mom is on her "fatten up Janey" rampage. The two huge shopping bags of groceries I lugged home last night weren't enough.

---

24 In fact I was an usher at the San Francisco Symphony while in high school. My flute teacher occasionally played in the orchestra.

Have you heard? Alice invited Mom to a fashion show this Saturday. So Mother has already made an appointment at the hair dresser's, etc.

October 4, 1960

Mary had the most ironic story this evening. It concerns Eddie Gregson (we rented his Palo Alto apartment for a while) and his party in New York. The guest list of about ten included Tony Perkins.[25] Being a celebrity, Tony, of course, was the last guest to arrive. In the meantime, Eddie had time to don the maid's black and white uniform and a wig, and borrowed the butcher's knife to surprise Tony at the door. Tony was so struck that he fainted dead away when he walked in. Serves him right, don't you think, for frightening us so in *Psycho*?

Yes, it will be a very good idea to start looking at staple household items, particularly in March or even during Thanksgiving. We don't have to decide, but it's fun just shopping around. Then when we do buy, we will know when we're getting a good buy and know what is good to have. When I'm up can we also sort of look at possibilities for a house? I'm anxious to meet your advisor, Dr. Soddy.

October 5, 1960

I really didn't mean to send you wine glasses for you to save. I wanted you to enjoy your wine in the correct containers. Snobbish me thinks that the wine would taste better that way. I also want you to make the final decision as to the crystal pattern, color, shape, etc. on the glasses we intend to collect. In fact, I bought a couple of those

---

25 In the Alfred Hitchcock movie *Psycho*, Tony Perkins was the psychopathic killer who stabbed a woman to death while she was taking a shower in a motel room.

glasses for us to use down here. So whenever you have wine or when I have the same, I can feel that you and I are enjoying it together, bound together by glasses. Pretty far fetched, I admit, but I want to think of you having gracious dinners.

And remember my saying that it is possible to have some nice things at very nominal prices? However, do you think it would be kosher if we initiated the glasses again when we are together? Since I've mentioned wine, it brings to mind a question. How could people possibly drink wine that has been contaminated with punch?

I talked to the most charming Danish girl who's married to a physicist who is over here for a year. She was very much the Grace Kelly type of person, only much warmer. I got the address of a Danish home furnishing shop (glassware, silver, furniture) to send for their catalogue. From that catalogue we can pick out the things we want and send back for them. It's so much more original this way and much cheaper. What do you think?

October 9, 1960
The fashion show and lunch at the Imperial Palace was very enjoyable. As usual I gorged myself on chow mein. Lil was sitting next to me and so there was my chance to learn her secret of keeping a balanced budget. Mother also spent some time talking to Lil, whom she thinks is one of the most charming and capable girls she's ever met.

October 19, 1960
I filled our beautiful spice jars last night. Our spices seemed to have been transformed into the most exciting ever condiments—yellow, green, browns. Many, many

thanks. I can't wait until the day when in <u>our</u> home there will be rows upon rows of these jars.

October 20, 1960

I'll be heading home after work tomorrow. I am anxious to sit down with the folks and give them more details of our plans.

I spent the lunch hour wandering through the House of Today store and paid special attention to crystal ware. I came to the following conclusion: although the design of German glasses is not as visually pleasurable as that of Swedish glasses, the ring is much sharper and clearer. So it must be that the glasses are of better quality. I thought you might be interested in the small enclosure. They only had one design from Germany but many from Sweden. The prices aren't too bad, are they?

October 23, 1960

Grandma and Aunt Alice are back from their Hong Kong trip and are laden with gifts and my trousseau. I was simply aghast at all the things I was getting. There is at least $400 [$3,600 in 2021 dollars] worth of Chinese dresses alone. Then there is jewelry, chests, etc. I can't imagine what I can possibly do with all those Chinese dresses, but Mom, since she had a good trousseau (she began selling her dresses when cash got low), insists that her daughter should have the same. Actually it's very nice even though there may be things we need more than simply keeping me warm.

There is just one thing I would like you to promise me, though. I'll go along with anything else often, but please, no long passionate kiss after the vows with the whole of

Chinatown watching. Just a thing that has perpetually disturbed me at so many weddings.

It's indeed sweet of your dad to invite the Youngs and all for Thanksgiving. That will really be an occasion of thanksgiving—to have you home, us together, and our families so congenial and happy.

10. Reconciling Our Differences

Religion

During Stanford's spring break in March 1960, Janey and I went on a three-day trip to Yosemite National Park with Ben and Ruth Hammett, our chaperones—an essential detail to placate our parents. On that trip we talked, for the first time, about having a serious relationship that would lead to marriage. After the trip, it seems that religion became an important topic in the letters we exchanged. Janey was baptized Catholic as an infant and was only recently confirmed into the faith, and her Catholic faith was very important to her. My parents belonged to the Chinese Methodist church one block from our home in San Francisco's Chinatown. I was baptized Methodist but was not a practicing member of the church. As a youth, I dutifully accompanied my parents to services at the church, which were conducted in Cantonese. My Chinese American mother spoke only English and so we only spoke English at home. Thus I had no idea what was happening or being said during the services at the Chinese Methodist church.

However, my view of Christianity was Protestant and Janey's was Catholic. If we were to be married, we needed to reconcile the differences between our religious views for our benefit and for our prospective children. I told her that I didn't know anything about the Methodist denomination because all the services I attended as a child were in Chinese. I also said that I was a classical musician and knew traditional Catholic music and that I had no problem with becoming a Catholic. After we were married, I was the organist at two New Jersey parishes, a music director at a Chicago parish, and a cantor at three parishes and at St. Patrick's Cathedral in New York.

March 28, 1960

You may find the rest of this letter rather confusing
and sporadic. I have so many thoughts running through
my mind and so must sort of piece together the pages
of mental letters. Hmmm. Long-term plans do seem
rather nice. But after reading your letter, I was suddenly
overwhelmed with a great sense of responsibility. As a
person I have a need for a complete-self type of feeling. No
more of that young girl sort of dreaming, floating thing.
Decisions are really now my very own. No more ready-
made plans that fall in a pretty pattern that I follow like a
good little girl.

You know, we really don't know each other very well.
I think we are people who have a hard outer shell which
is rather difficult to penetrate. I have been one who has
let few truly know me. Perhaps I'm sort of afraid of being
discovered. And then, to give of oneself is one of the
hardest gifts to give—but it is the greatest. However, once
given, it's one of these things that can't be taken back like
a material toy. So I have been very selfish with this gift.
It's funny, but I believe I do know you better through your
letters. They're so sensitive yet logical, so thinking, wise,
and soooo like a scientist.

I'm so sorry that Catholicism has caused you such
concern and worry. So typical of a Protestant!! As
I've mentioned before, I have just been introduced to
Catholicism, or rather to God. I was baptized a Catholic
as Mother was one. But according to the tenants of the
Church, she has probably been excommunicated many
times over. However, according to my ideas, she is a far
better Christian than many ritualistic Catholics who don't
eat meat on Friday and attend mass at 6:00 a.m. every

day without fail, 365 and a half days a year. As for me, I had been violently against the type of religion that my sister's godmother seemed to purport, i.e., down to Hell you go if you miss mass on a Holy Day just once! Then it suddenly clicked in my mind only recently that the important thing, faith and love of God—and it is a very, very personal love and belief—is never achieved through force or indoctrination. And again, it requires the opening of oneself and giving of oneself. I don't think that I've completely done that yet. I am still quite self-centered and selfish. To me Catholicism is a way of partaking in God's love, and I don't condemn others for participating in other ways. What I dislike most is dogmatism and preachers who try to convert the "heathen" to their way of worshipping and thinking. Perhaps I'm a pretty shaky Catholic but it doesn't seem to me that the religion should be so rigid and unyielding as most onlookers believe that it is. I was talking to Sara yesterday (she's a Protestant), and it was she who said that Catholicism does not deny a full life nor does it discourage one from questioning the beliefs of the Church. Actually, to accept all the laws and doctrine of the Church without question or conviction would indeed be a poor Christian.

As for the Pope, he is definitely not a divine messenger but is the executive head of the Church, like the head of the state. His job is to interpret and execute the law—the Scriptures—and he is infallible in so far as not defining the articles of faith which are against those taught by Christ and the apostles. However, it is possible for the Pope to sin or to make a mistake in judgement outside of matters on morals and faith. Also, the decrees of the Pope are actually a policy at a given time and situation and thus are often subject to fluctuations, but the doctrines of the Church are those set down only by Christ and don't change.

I do hope the above sketchy explanation will clarify a few things. But perhaps it would be easier if you give me some definite questions and I'll try to look them up and find some answers. I'm afraid that my theology is not particularly extensive and therefore I will need to do some research. I am most anxious to clarify any misconceptions, and it will also do me good to find what I believe in and why. Needless to say, I don't see why the question of religion always stands foremost in most people's minds. They sort of separate religion from the person, where it is an entirely different entity. To me, it's an integral part of the person, so although I haven't been a very staunch Catholic, religion is still what I am. And so if you do love me, religion has made me that person; and Catholicism is a way that I have found, so far, to express myself.

It's rather funny, but Dad was at one time a Methodist. He's not much of a churchgoer, in fact he spends his Sunday mornings over the comic pages. But nevertheless I consider him to be leading a rather good Christian life. There has never been any conflict in our family over religion, though at times it's hard to get Dad to go to at least Easter service with the rest of us. You know that bit about worshipping together as a family at least once a year, etc.

Concerning bringing up children in one faith or another, that is really an environment factor. However, to deny them exposure to the Catholic faith is probably just as much a crime as showing them only the Catholic way. No doubt too many religions will lead to much confusion and uncertainty, driving one into atheism or agnosticism.

Fortunately, in my mind, the basic tenets of most religions are the same. It's all a matter of what one was to do about it.

In my childhood I think I went to Sunday school in about ten different churches, from the Quakers to Baptist to Protestant, etc. Mother had many friends who wanted me to go in the right direction, but somehow the Catholic pull was the stronger. Many people feel that Catholicism is a too demanding religion. It appears so because it requires a more active participation than just sitting in church an hour each week listening to a preacher expound on how to be good. However, in Catholicism one partakes because one wants to, not because one fears the consequences (though that may be the reason for many people). Sometimes I feel I must obey a certain regulation, but that's because many things that Catholics do appear to be a joke to the Protestants and I sort of go along to keep all humored or just antagonize them a bit more.

So much concerning religion. I hope I didn't sound as if I were trying to preach or convert. I have no intention of doing that. I hope that explains me more clearly.

I am very pleased that you brought this question up. I do dislike situations and problems that are kept hidden and suppressed, causing great anxiety. Possibly my position will still cause you much concern, but that's how it stands. So there's still one question concerning the Church law that you suggested which I haven't answered. I am not sure of my stand, but am thinking about it. However, as I'm rather idealistic about certain things, I think that my conclusion will be somewhat in conflict with yours, though practically you are right. I am running out of words now so I will close. Off to classes—a hematology lab.

April 4, 1960

I am now in the lab waiting for the bacteria to grow.
They don't grow fast enough for impatient me. I was a bit
worried as to how you would have interpreted my stand on
religion. So many times what is so clear in my own mind
comes out rather twisted when it gets down on paper. And
even people who are very liberal may sound somewhat
dogmatic to others. And then, to believe in something, one
has to be firm. Thus I have been haunting the mailbox,
wondering whether I had gotten my intended point across.
I am glad you didn't mistake me for the Salvation Army
trumpet player.

April 17, 1960

Today was actually my biggest day. I took my First
Communion and therefore the full participation at mass.
John and Connie were so cute. They were so afraid that I
would panic and not do the right thing, etc. So although
they were sitting in the opposite aisle, they waited for
me to go up, John leading the way with Connie following
close behind so I wouldn't get lost. John was so concerned
that I would start chewing on the bread, but it got stuck
on the roof of my mouth and so there was nothing I could
do but wait for it to melt. The Communion is the most
beautiful thing ever. I'm so glad that I finally got around to
it. And Confession wasn't half as bad as I thought it would
be. I discovered that the priest isn't the disciplinarian,
etc. It was really just an examination of conscience and
contrition.

April 23, 1960

I'll have to explain Confession at another time. It's too

hard to get down on paper. But as for Communion and all, I was one who had very little to do with religion for a long time. In fact I was more an atheist. Then I was too lazy to learn about the Church until last fall quarter when I started going with my roomie. Fate brought two Catholics together and I began to take some instruction to prepare for Communion. I used to amaze my Jewish roommate last quarter with my faithful Sunday morning trek but she was pretty good about lending me her car. Excuse me for being dumb, but I didn't know that Methodists also had Communion. Then it was only recently that I learned what it was all about. Anyhow, I used to think it was a special biscuit given only to good people, i.e., the elite of the parish.

July 15, 1960

Richard, I wonder what we did to be able to deserve all this happiness. Now be sure to say your prayers every night.

August 15, 1960

I'm so glad you are coming home in two days. It's that feeling I am getting to know you as you are in letters. I'm sure that I can never quite express the precise feeling I feel when thoughts have to be put down in black and white. It isn't that I don't enjoy sharing my thoughts with you, but somehow in my own mind the paper words don't hit the same key as my singing! I was thinking of our last conversation and how we had to postpone talking about religion over the phone for fear that it would be misunderstood. I'm just so glad there are only two more days. Promise to be on time. West Coast #735 at 4:15 p.m. DST, right??

August 25, 1960

Yes, the weekend was too short for having lengthy
discussions, especially on the subject of religion. At
approximately 2:00 a.m. I had a talk with Anna last night
about the problem of the church wedding. I admit I was
not too coherent. But I did catch a few good suggestions,
though they were arguments for the Catholic Church and
talking to Father for guidance to contemplate. She had
just returned from a social visit with Father Tierney, and
between shooting the breeze she brought up the question
of first having the Catholic ceremony and then the "circus"
as you put it (a ceremony in the Stanford Memorial Church
on campus). It seems that part of the promise to the Church
is not to make our promises to one another before the eyes of
another Church. And even if we hold no value to the vows in
Memorial Church, the fact remains that we partook in the
ceremony before the hundreds of witnesses. i.e, idea vs action.

I can't demand that you give in to my beliefs. But
it is my conviction that a marriage is an act by God
and therefore must be performed in His presence. The
argument to you may sound as emotional as yours, but it
still remains that I have to be married in the Church or
else give up my religion. Richard dear, I'm floundering so,
not knowing what to do, and I love you so deeply. First
thing next week I'll talk to Father Tierney. I'm sure that
he can help us; he's very understanding. And of course, this
is one of the problems that he is always coming across as
he heads the Catholic Chapel for Stanford students, and
most are around the marrying age. There will be no double
wedding, and that's completely settled.

Don't worry about it too much now. It would be
much easier to talk about it when we see each other

again. And it also may clarify things (misconceptions) by talking to Church experts. But really, when people think of Catholicism they immediately think of "meatless Fridays" and "birth control," forgetting the most important elements, which is terribly unfair. They've condemned us even before giving us a chance. Let's leave this subject for a little while.

August 27, 1960

I was so happy that you finally called last night. I had great fears that my letter had disturbed and hurt you, although I hadn't intended to do so. But as the wedding fast approaches I felt that some statement should be made on how the situation stands, not trying to fool ourselves or avoid it in devious ways.

I am so proud of you for having to be absolutely willing and convinced before you make any promises. It will make whatever we finally decide on more meaningful and strong. You are so right when you say that you must be able to know that can fulfill your promises before you make them. And in the meantime I'll read up on your side of the argument. Con is working on an another angle with Father Liang, another very understanding Catholic priest.

August 29, 1960

That antenuptial agreement[26] certainly is worded so that one has the impression that one is signing one's life away. I find it comparable to police action by the Church to gain

---

26 Prior to Vatican II (1962–1965), a Catholic marriage between a Catholic and a non-Catholic required both parties to agree to raise their children in the Catholic faith. Janey, as the Catholic, seemed to over-react to what she calls the prenuptial agreement. I guess we signed it, but it was of so little consequence to me that I don't remember signing it.

new members and protect the ones they have. Basically this is useful both to the Church as well as to the Catholic spouse to give them a law to use in case one person objects to the other for continuing in his or her faith and raising the children as Catholic. Ideally, this argument would be necessary if one is a firm believer in Catholicism. One would naturally follow this course. It would probably hurt the Catholic member very much if he or she were prevented from practicing the faith. And also to receive a sacrament of the Church, e.g. marriage, one would, of course, want to reciprocate in loving God, etc. I think I object to signing that agreement as much as you do; it's a shame that people have so little confidence in human nature to have to resort to such a petty thing. But again, it's like any other law, for control, etc. I must admit I don't know all the laws and theories of Catholicism, being relatively new to the faith. But as I've said many times over, the real important question is loving God and living by his love, and in organized religion, like political parties, there are many "wings" within it. I agree with you—this is a good time to reexamine my personal beliefs and ideas. I hope that we will have time to do a lot reading between now and when you return. Then we can discuss our beliefs more thoroughly when we are together. Right now I feel my inadequacies in trying to explain many things. Also, I am interested in your ideas about religion.

October 17, 1960
I can't tell you how happy I am that you have resolved our church problem [and are willing to become Catholic]. It made me very sad that you would give in simply because you were forced to, sort of grudgingly. In that

way there would always be the spiritual gap. Really, the important thing is feeling the spirit of religion and not so much the more physical aspect and laws of it, i.e., the more trite stereotypes of Catholicism. There are many interpretations of the religion that I can't sincerely go along with, but as Bob and Sharon have said—and I think they have mentioned it again—it's the feeling of love and universality. And again, so much of it is what we have been brought up with and what is familiar to us.

October 19, 1960
No, your letter of the 18th didn't upset me at all. Your statements were fact and valid. Richard, don't think me so defenseless and naïve that you must protect me from your thoughts. I do want to know what your ideas are and where you stand on various issues, so that I wouldn't be at a loss trying to find a line to communicate with you. There are times that I feel like an outsider or intruder when you lapse into your silence because you think that what you have to say is too great a blow for me to withstand.

Then I know that I can't express myself very well much of the time, especially on the subject of Catholicism. Of course there is much about it that I don't yet know, but I did so want to share with you what little I know last Sunday when we went to church together. But somehow I had the feeling that you went with determination not to like it or even try to understand. And also, I was afraid that any explanation would sound like preaching as I was under the impression that you had enough church for the day.

However, I am beginning to see how much you want us together to share in giving our children a religious education. That was something I've never been very

conscious of as in our family each one goes his or her
own way to church. And even when we do go to the same
church, it usually ends with each one going at a different
time. Despite the different ways we spend Sunday, I
strongly believe that our basic attitudes toward God are
the same. So I do think that your role in teaching our Spot
and Puff to be Christians will be as important if not more
than my showing them a way to worship God. And what's
more, they don't have to attend Catholic schools. I'm all
in favor of the public school system, being a product of it
myself. The only thing that disturbs me about the public
school is the great number of "girls" they employ—ones
who go into teaching simply for the lack of anything better
to do.

October 23, 1960
Mom just burst with joy to discover that you consented to our
marriage in the Catholic Church. She always wanted it this
way but she disliked the idea that you should be forced into
it. Mother said that she suddenly feels a release of tension
and anxiety for she was so worried that the issue was
making you unhappy. Now you're an absolutely darling boy!
So grateful that you understand and want me to fulfill my
obligations. But Dad still says, "What's wrong with Stanford
Chapel?" Then we remind him that he didn't get married
there even though he could easily have. But most important
is what we make of our marriage after the ceremony.

November 15, 1960
I called Father T. this afternoon and went over for a
chat this evening. We chatted about things in general as
he guessed that we would have a large wedding in San

Francisco at Old St. Mary's. He thinks it's very impressive, beautiful, and very befitting.[27] I think I would ask him to officiate as he is the priest I know to a certain extent. I do want a personal touch and not just any priest who happens to be at the church. Father T. says he's looking forward to meeting you when you are down again, possibly during Christmas when it's less hectic at Stanford. So maybe we can have a social visit over dinner some evening. He suggests that we put in an order for the church right away, for if we are interested in St. Mary's, it's not too soon to apply. As for other details, they can be taken care of later. He gives me the impression that there's really no problem to it at all once I've found a man to marry (i.e., we don't have to apply all the way to the Pope for permission). I asked him about the children's education. He said there is no clause that binds them to a parochial school. The important thing is to include religious training as we see fit. However, Father T. says he's prejudiced but he thinks the parochial schools are better than the public schools, but again, that depends on the area where one lives.

November 28, 1960
You're far away again, yet after each visit I find you to be so much closer spiritually. Despite our forever having to be social creatures during our short weekends together, don't you think that those snatched moments alone were years of spiritual growth?

December 6, 1960
Thursday, I'll be going to visit Father Tierney. No

---

27 But St. Ann's Chapel in Palo Alto seats only 200.

particular business, just social. However, perhaps we can arrange a time to see him when you are here.

December 11, 1960

I met Father Liang, the Catholic priest, who was at the Chinese Students Conference, a rather nosy person who was most anxious to know of our plans, etc. and particularly gleeful that you consented to be married in a Catholic Church.

February 26, 1961

Mother knows her daughter's procrastination. With good intentions, I've been planning to write down to Whittier for my baptismal record. When I went in for more paper, I looked over her shoulder to find that she already gave up on me and is doing it herself. Oh, she's put me to shame. But I will see Father McGuire for sure this week to arrange our meeting with him, I promise.

February 28, 1961

When I go down to Palo Alto Saturday, I'll drop in to see Father T. and chat about the wedding and tell him of the new date, 7/9/61.

Finances

Janey and I were in complete agreement about the importance of financial planning for our married life. We were Depression-era children. I was born in 1937 and she in 1938. We shared stories of how our families struggled financially in the 1930s from the economic effects of the Depression, amplified by racism, which severely restricted our fathers' careers. The story uppermost in my mind is about a patient who paid my father during the Depression with one egg. In turn that single egg was fed to my brother, who was an infant at the time. In her letters Janey writes about crying herself to sleep listening to her parents arguing about their finances in an adjacent room.

We inherently knew, in the 1960s, that our career opportunities would be limited by racism. A PhD in physiology was not a ticket of admission to an assistant professor position at a top-tier university. Diversity of academic faculty was not a topic of significant consideration then, and this continues to be a struggle in the 21st century.

Our expectations were to achieve our individual academic goals, get jobs appropriate to our qualifications, have a family, prepare our children for college, and deal with racism issues that would undoubtedly arise wherever we lived. For example, I was asked in the 1980s to take a seat on a town council in New Jersey that was being vacated by a member who was moving to a new job. When my name was announced as the new council member, the New Jersey chapter of the Ku Klux Klan began a campaign against me, claiming I was a Communist. They didn't bother to do their homework. At that time, I was an advisor to the Minister of Economics in Taiwan—definitely not a Communist assignment. Janey forbade me to get involved in politics and to stick with fire fighting and EMS.

September 7, 1960

About investments, etc.—that has often come into my mind. Really that is the most practical thing we can possibly do. And it is the only way we can afford to live as well and hope to put our children through college. It has been the same in the case of our family. Dad's meager salary just barely keeps a roof over our heads and food in the refrigerator. Everything else has come from investments. For instance, without Kan's, I probably could never have gone to Stanford. But again, we've lost a small fortune in bad investments. The month before Dad got married, he took all his savings for a "sure thing" speculative stock which zoomed down the day before wedding, so he had to borrow money for the ring, etc. So in the long run the best deals are really the slow conservative stocks, i.e., Bell T&T. Seriously, we should invest in Bell T&T. Then we wouldn't feel as guilty making phone calls, knowing that we are supporting the company.

September 26, 1960
Mom would like very much for us to have enough for a down payment on a small cottage, so we wouldn't ever have to worry about the next month's rent. Or, as I noticed from your clippings, it might not be a bad idea to buy land near the university; then they would have to expand into our backyard and our land value will no doubt zoom sky high. Oh, I'm just a dreamer at heart!

On money, excellent idea to pool resources in a bank savings account. We don't need to wait until March, we can start now. I was planning to open a savings account soon anyway. I hate to be an iconoclast, but realistically, I seriously wonder whether we can really save much money before the wedding. After the wedding, moving to Oregon for you to start your graduate studies will make big dent in our finances. Mother was very consoling on this subject. If Kan's and Ming's[28] come through next year I may get some stock.

---

28 Ming's is the other Chinese restaurant in which Janey's father was a partner. It was in Palo Alto and became very popular with Stanford students, athletes, staff and faculty. The two restaurants were affiliates and expected to generate profits for Janey's family.

181

September 27, 1960

I opened a savings account today. I deposited $150 [$1,350 in 2021 dollars] with high hopes of keeping a fair portion in until the next paycheck. I also paid about $60 in back charge account bills, so that's one great pressure off and the new month appears to be getting off in the right direction.

October 1, 1960

After that last letter of yours, I've come to the conclusion that it's your turn to take some of the advice you've been doling out to me: relax, take it easy, and find peace in our love. I hate to see you worry as much about monetary matters. The only thing that we can do now is do our best to save and not let the subject of money produce such strain.

October 24, 1960

Finance and credit haven't been good anywhere else but at Magnin's[29] so I finally charged one ice bucket for the Van der Veldes. I hope it meets with your approval. Maybe we can get them something Chinese some other time. I didn't want to borrow from Mom when we were in Chinatown Saturday as she too was a bit tight toward the end of the month.

October 26, 1960

It's payday again. I feel that I can live again after paying bills. I just can't stand that feeling of having bills hanging over my head.

October 31, 1960

This evening over the phone you mentioned our being such

---

29 A luxury store in San Francisco, now closed.

extravagant people. I agree, but it's not that as much as being brought up around certain things and always before being able to buy certain things without giving money much thought. I find that my strange quirk is wanting what's good and not accepting substitutes. Lately though, I've discovered that substitutes are finding their place around me. Finances certainly are strong dictators. My firm stand on having only the best or nothing at all is crumbling! Then I forget financial status and go off and splurge again. But I do believe that a spurge every so often does wonders for one's morale. Perhaps you should set aside a section in our budget for splurges. It's easier to scrimp and save when there is a relief once in a while.

November 12, 1960
I hope you aren't upset that I endorsed your accepting money from your dad. But if it hurts your masculine pride too deeply, please don't do it. It just seems to me that when one is still going to school, one can never be totally independent. However, we can be that once we get settled next year. Also, what little breaks we can get now (when our parents still consider us under their wings and are so willing to help) will certainly ease our future situation. No matter what will be the case next year—my working or going to school—our finances will be very tight and we simply can't go running home when unexpected expenses arise. That's why it hurts me each time your bank account dwindles a bit lower. It's so much easier to accept the silver platter now when it's offered than to ask for it later.

Perhaps I'm being very selfish when I think this way. There's no doubt that our parents should enjoy what they have earned, but I don't think we're asking them to give up anything (except a few less drinks) when it's their idea to present a gift. Then again, it might be argued from the standpoint that you really don't have to make trips down during Thanksgiving or Christmas or that we don't have to make phone calls. But since we have made that decision we have also set the situation such that we are most susceptible to parental aid.

I'm very sorry to have brought up this touchy problem. So disregard it until you are in a good frame of mind. It's just silly little me who worries constantly about "coins." When I was younger I use to wake up in the middle of the night from Mom and Dad's shouting over money. So I don't want Spot and Puff to cry themselves to sleep to those same sounds and worry about matters that they really can't do anything about.

November 14, 1960
Good work, Richard, but it was so sweet of your dad to come through so well. I think that he understands the problems of a school boy in love (plane fares expensive?). I'm particularly glad you can now get the bank account cleared up.

The few greens I've stashed away for emergencies only will be coming in handy, That's my part of our joint account that I've started. It's a secret! Oops, I should not have told you.

November 16, 1960
Mom called a few minutes ago. They were so delighted with your letter. Since I didn't get a letter from you today, I insisted that Mom read your words to me over the phone. My parents accepted our invitation of the 27th

with pleasure. They said that they would pay for it but I insisted No! OK?

January 5, 1961
I'm so happy about your seven-hour job, because the time you have left for studying is more valuable than any research or teaching assistantship. As for financial problems, by February you can draw on our "mutual fund," so don't worry anymore about these trivials.

January 18, 1961
My parents are saying that it's too impractical for me to make a trip in February when we should be saving our coins for an auto. I'm having difficulty convincing them otherwise. And you may have to consider expenses for a trip to Illinois, Los Angeles, etc. This may have to be a time to be practical.

January 23, 1961
I'll soon be getting my paycheck and won't need to live on borrowed money. With the expenses of Christmas I would never have been able to survive if I had stayed in Paly this month. I also will be getting two extra sums of money from income tax returns and vacation pay coming from the Genetics Department. Each month I'll be giving $200 to Mom to stash away, so by June our little nest egg will be up to $1,200!! [$10,800 in 2021 dollars]. Enough for a fairly decent auto, though not for the dream Mercedes-Benz.

January 1, 1961
I received my first paycheck today and now I'm in the most celebratory mood. It's the great sum total of $333.98,

which is two cents less than my basic pay at Stanford. Oh, do I feel rich. But when I added up my unpaid bills of ~$150, I sadly realized how fast even great sums of money go. But with the help of that extra vacation money that Stanford should be sending up any minute now (if they still remember), I'll still be able to pay bills and save $200. By the way, how is your financial standing? If needed, our revolving fund will revolve up Oregon way.

After We're Married

For Janey's first visit with me in Eugene, Oregon, fellow graduate student Bob Van de Velde and his wife, Sharon, generously lent me their car for the duration of Janey's stay because my only mode of transportation was a bicycle. Janey was given a complete tour of the lab I worked in and invited to dinner with my advisor, Dr. Soderwall, and his family. However, it was the party with graduate students given by the Van de Veldes that turned Janey's thoughts to our future home and family. When we became engaged, I sent Janey a copy of the *Dick and Jane* books used to teach reading when we were in elementary school in the 1940s. Meeting the Van de Veldes' infant son, Gus, immediately reminded Janey of the children in the *Dick and Jane* books, especially when she saw me reading to him, something I did whenever I visited Bob and Sharon.

November 12, 1960
The sight of you reading to little Gus must have been all too delightful. It even more increases my desire to have children, and you can read *Dick and Jane* to them. Oh, so wonderful.

February 1, 1961

After being on the West Coast all of our lives, it would be an exciting change to live in the East and see the country a bit, don't you think? I understand that the Midwest can be quite a provincial place, but a place like Syracuse with New York just a stone's throw away should be more stimulating than San Francisco (that is, according to people from New York proper.) It also may be that I'm greatly influenced by romantic tales of New York and want to partake in a bit of the cultural activities. However, I would suppose that intellectualism flourishes on every college campus and it's up to us to make the most of it. But for you the East does have a great bulk of the scientists and you may not feel quite as isolated as you might at Oregon Medical School, where visitors who come may be more interested in the countryside.

February 1, 1961

So looking forward to mid-March, when you return to San Francisco and we can begin to make more definite plans for our life together so that I can see beyond our July 9th wedding a bit.

February 7, 1961

Last night's home decorating class was most fun. I like the concept of decorating, that is, to extend one's personality to one's living quarters, making a room enjoyable and suitable to what one's interest encompasses. For instance, the teacher suggested ways to set up a library in the bathroom to entertain those who don't have time to read elsewhere. We also got ideas on how to decorate on a shoestring.

Last night I had dinner with Julie from Hawaii. I got more advice on how to plan a wedding. She was married a year and a half ago and had a banquet for 700. She said that although everyone nearly had a nervous breakdown, she'd still do it the same way. According to her, the last week was worst, when every little problem became magnified 1000 times. In the end she simply set up committees and trusted her friends to come through. The solution seems to be good planning and not trying to do everything ourselves. We are lucky in that we have as much time as we do and have started now.

February 13, 1961
I saw the perfect set of pottery for everyday. It's from Formosa but designed by a California potter. A set of 53 pieces comes to $84 ($756 in 2021 dollars) and that's Gump's[30] prices. Now if we could get it direct we might be able to really get the price down. It looks very durable and is much more attractive than any plastic I've seen so far.

March 13, 1961
We are so much alike. A confession: I too keep a tab on all the Mercedes that I see going to and from work. I have decided that black, blue, or beige will do. Seriously, I do wish that I could stop looking at all of them and be a bit more realistic. Maybe our goal for 1970 after Spot and Puff appear on the scene? Then we could be the ultra conservative family.

February 17, 1961
Juliette was over for dinner while Mom and Dad had to go

30 A luxury home furnishings store in San Francisco.

out and I was left to entertain the guest. However, I still got the pep talk on the wonderful experience of married life. They were also very successful in their economic struggles. He was still going to school when they got married but is now working as a medical technician. She's teaching school and with their combined efforts they have purchased a house. Now salaries are very low in Hawaii, so comparatively I think we could manage very well on a California public health salary and then save your stipend. But then we will have to live far away from large cities, so I can't possibly go near a department store on Saturday.

February 21, 1961

You are the world's best mind reader. Only about three days ago I suddenly noticed the very nice lines of the new four-door sedan Volvos. And I further thought that its simple lines and contour resembled our dream Mercedes. But I dropped the idea, remembering how irate you were when I once mentioned that car—you thought they were like paper boxes on the highway. I must admit I was not especially infatuated with them in past years, except of course that they are serviceable. BUT when I saw the larger model just the other day, I was SNOWED! You're right, it'll serve the purpose well, for the time being.

February 22, 1961

The interior decorating class will be the greatest boon to our budget. Monday we learned about curtains. There are infinite little eye-deceiving tricks that can make the cheapest fabrics look elegant, so we learned. The course is completely geared for people like us starting off in possibly a small house or apartment on the barest of shoe strings. All we have to do is let our imagination run a little wild.

Sometimes I really get carried off in the deep end, as I now feel about our china. As much as I love it, I'm beginning to feel that it's as extravagant an idea as our Mercedes. What do you think? Or do you think that about four place settings will suffice to satisfy our whims and then invest in something more practical?

February 27, 1961

Mother is one of those people who is always saving things for special occasions or for her children, and when she's purchased something it is never seen again. But we'll use our china every so often, won't we? I also think that it is possible to lose much of the enjoyment and significance of material objects when one is too overly careful and cautious in their use.

February 26, 1961

I do think girls as a whole take children in stride more so than males. That is, they are more aware of the 150 diapers a week and feeding every three hours. That's part of our training when we started playing with dolls. But of course real live children are entirely different.

February 27,1961

I have a bit of bad news: your fiancée will never make a good parasitologist. Looking through the microscope gave me the worst case of motion (not morning) sickness. How I can live through these next two weeks of looking through the scope eight hours a day will be somewhat a miracle. Nevertheless, I can understand how dreadful the first few months of pregnancy must be with morning sickness. But it seems unfair that I should get a dose of that feeling when it's as unproductive as reading slides. This rocky bus ride isn't helping matters so I have to close before something comes up.

February 28, 1961
Among the many things I thought about today (while searching slides for anedea) was the place to live for us, two by two. Perhaps the type of place we live in is more important than we credit it. That is, it should be a comfortable place with lots of room, even if it's only an apartment. I was comparing the difference and changes in Mary's and my attitude after we moved into the smaller apartment. Whenever we turned we seemed to be in the other's way and at least once a week our nerves simply gave out. People just need room sometimes to think and be by themselves. And the more inconveniences, the greater the number of chances for blowup. The adjustment to marriage is enough without cramped quarters to contend with. What I really mean is that I don't care how old and grubby the place may be, just so long as there is lots of closet room and a large kitchen. At 737 Waverley the atmosphere was less oppressing and our tempers were kept at a much lower level. I have passed our order to Mom for a vacuum cleaner and Osterizer.

March 12, 1961
Last night Cuz George and family were over for dinner. I am getting George's advice on buying a car. He says to shop around—the deals that one can get now are amazing. One could probably get a Chevy Biscayne for $2300

[$20,700 in 2021 dollars]. I asked what he thought about the Volvo. His opinion was that it's the best in it's field on the market. He would get that if he were buying, but one must also consider the cost of maintenance on foreign cars, which is the major cost of an auto. He also believes in upholding the American economy by purchasing the home-grown goods. He further suggested that if we were interested in a GM auto to go at the end of the month when they are slashing prices to meet their sales quotas.

11. Getting to Know Our Parents

When we finally announced our engagement to our parents and families in August 1960, there was a sigh of relief from both families that we were marrying within our Cantonese culture of the Pearl River Delta adjacent to Hong Kong. Our wedding would be Catholic, in San Francisco's imposing former and historic first cathedral, and spoken in English and Latin. The majority of the attendees were Chinese, not familiar with the rituals of a Catholic wedding, and many spoke Chinese as a first language. However, no part of the wedding ceremony included any reference to Chinese culture. As Janey's letters suggested, we needed to be gentle, solicitous, and aware of the different perspectives of our parents regarding the challenges of being sensitive to the diverse cultural views of the more than 1,000 guests—American, Chinese, and Chinese American.

My father immigrated from a Chinese village to San Francisco at the age of 15 and spent his formative teenage years working as a houseboy in American households in various California cities before earning his B.A. and M.D. at Stanford. He lacked basic social skills—Chinese or American. My mother died in 1955 and my father went to Hong Kong several years later and was introduced to Alice by his Stanford classmate and closest friend. He married her in Hong Kong and she emigrated to the United States in 1959. Her father was a civil servant and she was raised in a household with servants. Alice was an amateur painter and socialized with China's artistic elite, including Chang Dai-chien, known as the Picasso of China. He painted Alice's portrait, which now hangs in my apartment. Alice was fashionable, elegant, and charming, and spoke English as a second language. She quickly adapted to the Chinese American culture of our families but was still culturally Chinese.

Janey's father was raised in a traditionally Chinese household and yet was culturally Chinese American. Her mother was schooled in

China during her youth but was uniquely modern and a feminist, and she used whichever aspects of American or Chinese culture she thought appropriate at the moment for her purposes. She was the only Catholic among the four parents, but she practiced Catholicism in her own unique way.

From my own experiences as a parent and deacon, I would say that children don't really know or understand their parents until the children have had enough life experiences to appreciate their parents' perspectives and lives. The same can be said of parents whose children go off to college and return home as young adults and are expressing their first taste of independent life. In our fast-paced long-distance courtship, from our first significant date to our engagement in six months, Janey and I were intensely focused on each other and—to be honest—totally oblivious to what our parents thought. Now we had to adapt to the reality that our parents intended to put on and pay for Chinatown's biggest social event of the year. We were mere pawns in our parents' all-inclusive and complicated plans, from the design of the wedding invitations to the reception after the wedding.

July 13, 1960

I turned on the radio for the first time tonight to hear what was happening in the outer world, especially the Democratic National Convention[31] (we still haven't gotten our newspaper after 101 phone calls). We didn't listen long enough to understand all the proceedings. As we were concentrating so hard on our chess game, the shouting began to drive us simply out of our minds, so off went the set and we live further in ignorance. Nothing interests me less than politics. I am too lazy to try to keep up with all the maneuvers. But we were bought up in a Republican

---

31 John F. Kennedy was nominated for president and Lyndon Johnson for vice president.

atmosphere and have been conditioned and trained to love Nixon. What's more, he's from my hometown, Whittier. And then there is Kennedy, who is Catholic. Can you suggest an unbiased way for me to study presidential candidates? On politics (as everything else, including religion) you will get along perfectly with Dad—he's the most conservative Republican imaginable. However, there is a glint of that army imperialistic attitude in him still.

July 31, 1960

Went up to San Francisco as planned yesterday afternoon. Met Mother and some of her clan for dim sum at Heung Ah. I wished you could have seen the expressions on the faces of my aunt and grandma when mention was made of their trip to Hong Kong. They literally beamed excitement. Grandma kept saying how very much she would have liked me along, how proud she would be to return to China accompanied by her granddaughter, and a Stanford graduate at that. Oh, you know how conscious the old folks are about reputation and all. But she stoically accepted Mother's statement about your not liking it if I went. Anyway, my parents can't very well afford to give me such a trip, although I would love taking my grandma around. It is probably because she's so tiny and looks so helpless with her little bound feet that I feel a bit protective towards her. I've always admired her strength and intelligence, bringing up eight children by herself after her husband died. And I think, with great prejudice, that she did a particularly fine job with Mother.

My parents are very excited about the trip north. I've instructed Mom to be sure to include a bottle of soy sauce for you. Richard, how can you possibly cook without soy sauce? That's absolutely unheard of, and you're Chinese at that. Golly, soy sauce makes the difference in any cooking, especially hamburgers. They were pleased with your letter. They must have analyzed every word with the greatest scrutiny. Mom instructed me to tell you that she probably wouldn't have time to answer (she writes several drafts too) as they're packing. They should be in Eugene either on Monday or Tuesday (week after next).

August 8, 1960
Yes, I was terribly amused when Dad answered the phone Friday. The phone had been ringing incessantly since we returned home and by the time you called we were somewhat tired of being an answering service. So at the time you called, Dad said he would really give it to the party on the other end. But when he heard you he immediately mellowed. Amazing, isn't it? It makes me very happy that our relationship is so pleasing to our folks.

August 9, 1960
What heavenly communications from Oregon way last night and this morning. I heard from you and my parents both times. They sounded as if they are having the most wonderful time up there. A short insert from Con told me that she had a "blast" at the hamster lab, and your lab and office passed inspection. I expect to get full details when they return. Mom said that she really enjoyed meeting you and that you were a very good host. And she further commented on your being so much more poised.

August 15, 1960
It's been very pleasant spending the day at home. A change

of scenery even in the grey, dreary fog belt of San Francisco can be refreshing. And home is always comfortable. Mom has never been an efficient housekeeper, but nevertheless her loving charm fills the house. After finally waking up I attempted to put the house in order so that a clean house will greet a tired family from their long trip.

August 24, 1960
Do wish I could have seen your plane off Tuesday (sort of a change from the Oakland train station). However, I am most glad that you had the opportunity to talk to your father without interruptions (or, were you driving?).

August 27, 1960
Dad has been rather tired this last week, recovering from the excitement of our engagement announcement as well as taking over the work of his helper who was injured. So yesterday he decided to take off and swish mom away on a second honeymoon, leaving all the children behind to fare for themselves. They sounded so darling. Dad and Mom are staying in the hotel where they spent their first night, and again they registered as honeymooners. I'm so happy when each day they seem to grow more and more in love.

September 6, 1960
Mom called a few hours ago. She's so pleased that you, at least, have a cool head on your shoulders when we are together. Oh, what praises she showered on us! So good of your professor to write that letter to the other naval place. After looking over the pamphlet briefly, I honestly think you have an interesting six months down here.

September 25, 1960

I so wish that you were here to witness the cutest sight in the world. Dr. H. D. Cheu and J. C. Young in their shirtsleeves, completely exhausted from rooting for their Stanford team, which never made it, coming to pick up one lab technician, Janey Young, at 2469 High. Boy, were they in good moods despite the loss. I think it was getting back in the old college spirit that does so much for one's countenance. In fact, your dad at one point of the game was so excited that he found himself rooting for the wrong team.

So we sped up to San Francisco with your dad at the wheel and my dad acting like a little boy seeing skyscrapers and freeways for the first time in his life, craning his neck left and right so as not to miss a single flagpole. He admits he'd discovered many new wonders as a passenger. Per usual, the men got to the restaurant, Nam Yuen, before the ladies. The dads must have gotten a big kick out of having Chinatown seeing them walk down the streets "ensemble" with me in the middle. Every so often, there would be a "Hello, Doc!" "Hi John!" but I went unnoticed. The second they got in the restaurant, and seeing that the womenfolk were late, they headed for the beer barrel at the bar. This I wasn't supposed to notice, but I did—"apple polishing" people. The bartender when they ordered beer first reached for the glasses and good ole California Lucky Lager. Then he turned around, thought a moment, returned the Lucky and reached now for Millers. Pretty sly, don't you think?

Can you possibly guess what the girls were doing while the men were suffering under that hot, blistering sun? Yep, they were tucked away in the dark, air-conditioned comfort of the Nob Hill Theatre taking in *The Apartment* and *Happy Anniversary*. Alice and Mom felt that they too should have some entertainment while the men were away, so Alice called Mom that morning and arranged their date. Mom meanwhile hurried down to my aunt's to pick up a few more Mandarin phrases to use on Alice. And surprisingly she got her ideas across.

Your father, after a few beers, scotch and soda, and bourbon and soda (I couldn't see how his stomach could take such mixtures), was simply adorable. Before the girls got there, I learned all about you as a little boy, as well as playing the flute at graduation. Another funny story was one he told my dad about how your mom tricked the Southern Pacific Railroad into running a special train for the Stanford game.[32]

A very full evening (that lacks only you) of drinking, eating, and talking from about 6:00 to 9:00 p.m. I just couldn't help thinking about how lucky we are—such congenial future in-laws as well as such good parents. And I wonder just how many in-laws in Chinatown would be seen lunching together and then heading for a football game—and rooting for the same team?

October 1, 1960

A typical family dinner together at home with my parents. I had intended to spend the rest of the evening with the family chatting and then writing you without a single disturbance. But without fail, someone came. R. T., who just heard of our engagement, had to personally offer his congrats etc. as well as discuss his social life with Mother. Oh, Father was very annoyed as he was looking forward

---

32 She called Southern Pacific Railroad so many times they thought a lot of people wanted to take the train from San Francisco to Palo Alto for the football game. Mom and I virtually had the entire train to ourselves.

to spending an evening with his children and catching up on their intended plans. Dad almost got hysterical with laughter when R. T. came across a live wiggly worm in his apple. Said he, "That little worm didn't eat too much." After calling you, Dad has black specs on reading his autographed copy of Maderis's new book, *Countdown for Decision.*[33] Perhaps it's along the line of your "psychology of flight," but this is the old army point of view.

October 9, 1960

You'll find this hard to believe, but Mom is taking Alice to her calisthenics class. Mother is so sold on these exercises that she feels it's a cure-all for any ache and pain. But truly she has been more active and less tired since she's been exercising.

She amazed me with her cooking six courses for eight people in a matter of minutes last night with only a few minutes previous notice. But lately she adores entertaining young people. It's probably that she understands us more than we understand ourselves, and then too, she enjoys learning the experiences that the youth "suffer" through. It sort of gives her a share in their youth. And the young men flock to her.

November 6, 1960

Father and I clashed Friday night. It's amazing how much alike our temperaments are. We both are so stubborn and tactless and so unyielding. Poor Mother and Mary just sat petrified with awe as Dad and I pounded on each other, getting more and more unreasonable. I had promised Mary

---

33 In *Countdown for Decision* (1961) Major General John B. Medaris told "the powerful inside story of men, missiles and our race for space—by the man who launched America's first satellite."

that I would drive her over to Berkeley Saturday morning,
but Dad wanted me to go over with him to the Nixon
rally in Oakland as he was on the committee for getting
a Chinese delegation, complete with drum corps and all,
over there. Once Dad gets an idea he is so inflexible and
unyielding. He began accusing me of never doing a single
thing he ever wanted me to do and the rally was very
important to him and for the country as well, and I wasn't
doing my duty as a good citizen. He wouldn't even hear
of my first driving Mary to the University of California
at Berkeley and then meeting him at the rally because
I would not be able to find them in the great crowd. But
we both calmed down after catching a second wind and I
climbed up on his lap and used Mother's tactic of sweet
calm talk and explanation of my duty to my first promise
(as Mary doesn't know the way to the university).

So Saturday morning Mary and I crawled out of bed
at 7:00 and drove over to Berkeley. After seeing her to the
testing center, I wandered through Berkeley a bit and was
tempted to go with the Young Republicans' sponsored bus,
but they didn't leave until 10:45 and I thought it wouldn't
do if I were late and couldn't find Dad. So I took the bus
down to Oakland, allowing myself two full hours to search
through the crowd. But hardly anyone was at the square.
Then the rain started to come down in buckets. I ducked
into the first drugstore, then dashed back into the rain
and came across a dimestore type of place that sold foreign
imports of every imaginable shape and size. After leaving
the domain of exciting exports, I decided to stick to a good
ole American store and came across an umbrella sale.

I left and made my way through the crowd looking for
Dad, which as he said was like looking for a needle in a

201

haystack. Then I spotted a banner for Nixon written in Chinese, so using that as the guide I pushed and plowed my way through and saw Dad sort of standing a bit off to the side by himself. So I sneaked up from behind and took his arm. He must have been disappointed that it was only me and not one of those cute little "Nixonettes" passing out buttons.

Poor Dad really got it from Mom all the way across from Oakland, admonishing him for forcing his daughter to rush about so in the rain. Yup, family is back in harmony. Dad's happy again, but Mom says he has to pay for the umbrella I purchased.

As I told you, I took *Fun with Dick and Jane* home and Mom and Dad got a great charge out of it. It brought back memories of us as children struggling through first grade. I remember how much I loved some of the stories in that book. We must save it for posterity even if they no longer use it in school. Wouldn't they make good bedtime stories?

We got on the subject of the high cost of college these days and my parents then said we would have a handful of problems when Spot and Puff start college. I was stunned that they actually called our children Spot and Puff. What's more, they think it's so cute. Hmmph!

November 12, 1960
Mom and Dad came down to Moffett Field for a dinner dance with old army friends. Cute little Mom called between courses and after dinner because she could talk for as long as she wanted for only ten cents. She then proceeded to give me a lecture on how much I must take care of my "dear boy" and then how I must guard my health to prepare for Spot and Puff. Apparently M's wife's

miscarriage has troubled her somewhat. She had to babysit their daughter for an hour and she found that all too exhausting. Dad asked her what she will do when she has her own grandchildren. Mom flippantly answered, "When the time comes I can certainly handle my own."

November 20, 1960
I just talked to your dad and Alice. I thought I would check on whether or not I should prepare something for Thursday's dinner. Both sounded as if they were in good humor despite the Stanford Indians' loss yesterday. And also they're expecting us for dinner Wednesday.

November 28, 1960
Weren't our family dinners wonderful? Thanksgiving at your home, Mom and Dad's anniversary. My parents were certainly pleased and so proud to celebrate their 23 years of marriage surrounded by their children and two more to-be members. I still can't get over how fortunate we are that our families are so compatible. That has certainly removed any possible problems for us, don't you think?

December 1, 1960
I called Mom to wish her a happy birthday! She was just thrilled with your sweet card from her "dear boy." Your gesture meant so much to her. She said that she'll drop you a line in a few days. Don't worry, it'll be a type of letter that you wouldn't have to answer.

January 8, 1961
My visit at your home lasted longer than I anticipated as it ended in my having dinner with your dad and Alice. All were

in a good mood. I was very much amused when your dad got so excited the minute he started to talk about old times. When I mentioned to him that you sounded much happier about your work this quarter, it surprised him and he went on to say that although you're his son, he doesn't know how you feel or what you think at times. Well, I now bestow on you a medal as good actor in ability to disguise your feelings. I'm in very much the same predicament when it comes to my dad because he reacts to things much differently than I do and his criteria for importance have another baseline.

January 12, 1961
Your father called last night, prompted of course by your airmail letter. When I last saw him he mentioned that he thought it was silly of you to spend three cents more for airmail when both arrive at the same time.

January 25, 1961
Your dad called. Your friend Benny invited them for dinner on February 25th and I'm included also. Wasn't it dear of him to remember your fiancée? However, I do admit I'm getting a bit frustrated with attending functions with your family, as much as I love them, without you with me. In fact, I'm beginning to believe that I've spent more time with your family than with you. That is, it feels that way and I trust my emotions.

February 15, 1961
Dinner with Grandma last night was enlightening to say the least. At 87 she has the most remarkable memory and store of "goodie" information. I learned more about your family that you probably haven't even heard! Did you know

that your grandfather's first wife threw a great fit when your grandpa chose to take your grandma (the second wife) back to China instead of her? And one of your uncles was adopted in China because the true son got sick over there? Anyway, the stories were most interesting! Oh, one more goodie that amused me: your grandfather owed my grandfather $100 that has never been repaid. I think that the merger on July 9th will solve that problem, don't you?

February 20, 1961

You would have loved the festive atmosphere of Chinatown—the family associations[34] throwing their annual parties, out-of-town Chinese flooding the streets, flowers and oranges lining the sidewalks, and every so often a contraband firecracker blows up. Well, Dad and I spent a good part of the afternoon just strolling up and down Grant Avenue. We even followed the Miss Chinatown contestants up to one of the family associations, where everyone gave speeches but no one listened. Dad was so busy gossiping that he didn't realize that the president of the Chinese Chamber was introducing him to the meeting. I've never thought much about the family associations and was so impressed to find a huge room with marble floor and massive teakwood furniture after climbing three flights of narrow rickety stairs. I further was taken aback when one of the elders of the family association waddled over to serve me a cup of tea. Quite an experience.

34 Family associations are one of several types of organizations in China that provide a connection between a sojourner and his place of origin. They have existed in Beijing since as early as the 15th century CE. The general term for these associations is *huiguan*, meaning meeting hall. There are surname, dialect, county, and regional huiguans. They provide a place of support, food, and shelter for merchants and individuals who are away from home. (Him Mark Lai, *Becoming Chinese American: A History of Communities and Institutions*, Walnut Creek, CA: Alta Mira Press, 2004, p. 40.)

Your unassuming fiancée has been going around through the day wearing that angelic little halo over her head! Well, yesterday instead of working like a good student, I decided to be a good granddaughter and take my grandma out to the cemetery to her daughter's grave. That's almost the only thing that Grandma appreciates most as no one else in the family will take her out. Well, it's a one-day effort. One plans to start early and get it over with, but Grandma isn't ready until after noon. Then one must stop first in Chinatown to pick up cookies for the lady who owns the florist shop. The present of cookies will reduce the flowers to 50 cents and at the florist she's like a buzzing little bee, hopping from one type of flower to another, pulling a pink one here, a yellow one there until there is enough to fill a small vase. Then at the site, Grandma lugs out her gardening bag complete with scissors, cleaner, and watering can and starts to work. The ground is still wet from the last rain but she insists on watering all the plants. The shrubs are trimmed—I use a small pair of dissecting scissors—and the soil is turned with an old Chinese cleaver. Everything is done in Grandma's prescribed quaint ways. So I guess that's why no one is anxious to spend an afternoon this way. My enjoyment comes from talking to her and digging into the history of her Lee family side and I also manage to try out my meager Chinese.

When you are back in March, perhaps you can try again at my other grandma's friendship. I find her a very amusing person if one overlooks some of her idiosyncrasies, and she has quite a few.

February 26, 1961

Enclosed is my parents' New Year's greeting and lai shee.[35] This is the last we will be receiving. After we're married we will have to be the distributors.

We should not be afraid to use the "prized possessions." Their value is our enjoyment and shouldn't be kept stored in cases in the basement. Mother is one of those people who is always saving things for special occasions or for her children, but once she's purchased something, it is never seen again. But we'll use our china every so often, won't we? I also think that it is possible to lose much of the enjoyment and significance of material objects when one is too overly careful and cautious in their use. In that, Mom and Dad have been very good. I've broken so many of their objets d'art, yet they have always been more worried that the incident would frighten me than about the breakage itself. It's their philosophy that the material things can always be replaced and if not, what does it really matter?

---

35 Good luck money for children.

12. Preparing for a Cathedral Wedding

In the 1960s, nearly all Chinese Americans in San Francisco were restricted to living in the city's segregated Chinatown which was, for all intents and purposes, a Chinese enclave with a mélange of three cultures: Chinese, American, and Chinese American. Nearly all the Chinese emigrants to the United States before World War II originated from villages of the Pearl River Delta. They brought with them cultural concepts and practices. An important wedding ritual involved a comparison of the genealogy of the two families represented in a marriage between the bride and groom from different villages. Each village maintained a genealogy record of every family, a practice continued into the 21st century. The record is known in Cantonese as a *juk pol* (朱克波爾). The genealogy record for our village showed that my father was in the 29th generation of his family and the family lineage was being continued by my marriage to Janey. This fact made our marriage culturally important to the residents of Chinatown, especially the older generations.

This was the largest Chinatown wedding in 1961 and was particularly significant because if was between the children of two prominent Chinatown leaders, Col. John C. Young and Dr. Henry D. Cheu. The marriage also made a statement about educational achievement in San Francisco's Chinatown. The newlyweds and their fathers were graduates of Stanford University in a community where higher education was highly regarded culturally but out of reach for most Chinese American youths at the time.

The wedding took place in a historic religious landmark, Old Saint Mary's Cathedral, built in 1854 and San Francisco's first Catholic cathedral. It was a church familiar to most of our wedding guests but many had never entered it before nor attended a Catholic wedding. The 400 wedding invitations were treated by the recipients as something to boast about to friends and family. As was tradition at the time, each invitation was treated as an invitation to the invitee's family. At our wedding, the church was packed to the rafters with the invitees and their family members. The wedding party was appropriately large and included five bridesmaids, five groomsmen, and several ushers. The reception was held across Dupont Street (now Grant Avenue) and occupied all four floors of a restaurant. It was the hottest day of the year, the champagne flowed freely, and many of the guests who didn't normally drink alcohol gladly consumed the thirst-quenching bubbly beverage. Janey and I later learned that a number of tipsy guests tumbled down the grandly carpeted stairs between each floor. We left the reception as quickly as decorum allowed to begin our journey to Portland, Oregon, and graduate school for both of us.

Janey's letters are an effort to share with me the excitement and joy of the many events and activities preceding our wedding, all of which I could only attend vicariously through her letters. In her letter of August 29th, she meets my adopted family, the Chesbros.

August 29, 1960

The party, as you can well imagine, was really wonderful, but we (I in particular) wished you were there. I especially enjoyed seeing the Chesbros again—they are such fine people. I enjoyed talking to them, wishing though that I could have spent more time with them. I also like Aileen very much, but didn't have much time chatting with her. You know parties, and how one feels that one should spread oneself evenly with all of them. There were cocktails from 5:30 to 8:30, then a scrumptious dinner at Kan's (keeping the business in the family?). The menu was nearly identical to one we had last week.

Grandpa Cheu was so funny trying to pick up slippery abalone with chopsticks. He insists on inventing ones with sharp prongs at the end. Then he started talking about

209

Gilroy, and it turns out that the Chesbros are great friends of the Youngs down there. They are distant relatives of ours. When we were children Dad was always taking us down there to play with their chickens. Did you by any chance do the same? That makes me feel an even closer relationship with you.

October 1, 1960

This afternoon I wandered through Gump's and took another look at our Brastoff china. I was hunting around for crystal and antiques. But it's never as much fun as shopping with you. I am so anticipating Thanksgiving and exploring the shops of Eugene together.

From your description I get the visual impression that Eugene is gradually growing into an up and coming cosmopolitan city in certain aspects—just so long as they have cheese stores and a symphony orchestra every so often. I'm very excited about living in a still-quiet college town just like the one I was born in, provincial but friendly. A delightful country to bring up Spot and Puff. How nice it would be not to have to play on rooftops in Chinatown as I did in my ninth year.

October 24, 1960

Each time I think about our wedding I get more and more excited. Then I recall the weddings I have been in where I started to giggle when the tension got too great. At times of stress I notice the strangest things. The first time I nearly choked from trying to suppress laughter when I noticed the groom as he was kneeling and showing two huge shining horseshoe taps on the heels of his shoes. Then at N's wedding while walking down the aisle and looking at the guests, I looked around and suddenly noticed that the bride was wearing the very dress I had just purchased for high school graduation the day before. What will you do with a girl with such a strangely working mind?

It was indeed sweet of your dad to invite the Youngs for Thanksgiving, to have you home, us together, and families so congenial and happy.

October 31, 1960

I have been thinking about a church to get married in. Although it's much nicer in Palo Alto, it may be rather complicated because of the distance. I would need a place to get changed and there is the problem of time. I remember my cousin's wedding where the I. Magnin bridal consultant did all the wardrobe details. So much was expertly taken care of, but even there, a part of the attire was misplaced and poor Mother rushed down to Stonestown for a replacement. Thank goodness the store was only two blocks away. Also, most of the guests will be from San Francisco, and knowing San Francisco people, anything more than ten blocks away is too far. Not only that, but Mother is always the worrywart when people have to drive. She feels a personal responsibility for their safety until they reach home, even when it's from one section of San Francisco to another.

Personally I would prefer the peninsula and to have the reception at Ming's. But since the day will be hectic enough, I just wonder whether it would be wise to add another frantic factor. Well, we can discuss it further when you get back and we find a church you approve of.

November 10, 1960

I'm planning to do some shopping in preparation for
marriage, looking for crystal and china. Have we decided
definitely on the Brastoff Dynasty pattern? Each time
I go by Gump's I feel that I must stop and drool over it.
Actually, it has grown on me so much that I feel that it's
already mine. I need of course your absolute consent first,
and furthermore, we need generous friends.

December 1, 1960

I heard something of interest on the radio last night.
Did you know that in Virginia one can get married via
telephone as long as one member of the couple is speaking
from Virginia?

December 4, 1960

My parents and I didn't talk too much about our wedding.
My parents are waiting to hear from us about what we
want. However, they insist on having 400 seats on their
side of the church. By the way, dearest Richard, have you
officially asked Dad yet???!!!

December 7, 1960

I've finally decided on what I would like to wear, as in the
picture in the enclosed newspaper ad—if you have the
nerve to show up at the lingerie department.

December 11, 1960

On the subject of our wedding, Mom and I gave it some
thinking, but were completely at a standstill as to where
we can possibly hold the reception as Kan's is simply too
small and Ming's is too far away. Victory Hall I simply

can't tolerate, especially being part of long waiting lines, shoving crowds, etc. I wonder if it is much more to rent a room at hotels and then have our own Chinese caterer. No chow mein though! It's really a sad predicament that Chinatown has no nice halls for receptions, except perhaps when the Buddhist temple is completed.

January 7, 1960

I had a very nice talk with your friend, Cynthia. In fact, I learned quite a bit from her about wedding arrangements. She must have had boundless energy to get a wedding ready in a month and still work. The complicating factor was old-fashioned parents, so there were such things as pouring tea, cookies, roast pig, two receptions, and a banquet. She said that if she had to do it over again it would never happen this way. Isn't it nice that our parents aren't old-fashioned? That will certainly lessen the load of our possible problems.

I ran into my cousin's wife yesterday. She wasn't buying anything so we had a good chat. She told me she didn't believe it when people first told her that marriage was really the beginning of one's problems. But she said that God must have made engaged couples look at the world through blissful starry eyes, believing that they can easily overcome what difficulties might arise or else people would never get married. Nevertheless, I agree with your idea of it being more enjoyable to tackle problems together.

January 12, 1961

The day set for the "summit" talks is this Sunday beginning over cocktails at 4:00 p.m. I'm a bit petrified having grownups talk about us when you're not here to

213

support our point of view. But being practical and sensible people who have survived through raising us, I'm sure that they'll come to a reasonable agreement that will please both sides. One important question: are you absolutely positive about June 25th? The date, that is, getting married???

I have been thinking that it would be nice to live in a large city (good sized at least or else close to a large city) to take in exhibits, symphonies, etc. There have been so many things I've wanted to do in San Francisco and never had the energy to do it by myself. Hearing the girls at work talk has stimulated my craving.

January 16, 1961
I will give you a blow by blow account of the meeting of the wedding organizers on the six-month anniversary of our engagement (quite incidental?). However, before I forget, I had a guard put on my ring so that it no longer slips. It arrived yesterday at "Summit 1171 Pacific Ave" promptly on the nose—Daddy's military efficiency, you know. Orders were taken for drinks, each found a comfortable chair, drinks were brought in, and your Dad came dashing out with the hot clam cream cheese hors d'oeuvres. The meeting was called to order and the first item on the agenda was the date. I announced that June 25th was the date you're set on but presented the difficulties. Therefore it was the problem of convincing you that a later date might be more advantageous. Then ring ring and you were on the line (very clever). I was so pleased that you were agreeable and I proceeded back to the conference to announce Wednesday, July 9th.

As soon as the date was announced Lil again reminded me to arrange for the church tout de suite! In the interim I was on the phone. The conference had approached the subject of the type of reception to give. After some discussion—not much—they decided that the older Chinese wouldn't stand for scrimpy things like hors d'oeuvres. That is, they don't know how to appreciate the finer delicacies. And our family name would be mud in Chinatown. We really can't escape the social pressures as both our parents depend on Chinatown for a living and the wedding is as much their party, if not more so, than ours.

Practically speaking, if we had our own caterer we would have to rent a hall, whereas if we employ the services of the Four Seas restaurant we will get food as well as their army of waiters and dining room. The fault of the majority of the Chinese weddings has been their lack of good service, resulting in long, long lines, balancing paper plates, etc. A nice but simple buffet was agreed upon, minus the (usual) spareribs, chow mein, and greasy fried chicken bones.

The cake, flowers, etc. will be taken care of on our side. However, according to Emily (at Public Health), you are responsible for my bouquet and flowers for the mothers and the ring. Are you sure, are you absolutely positive that you don't want a ring?? This is your second chance.

All that time I sat and listened quietly. I couldn't possibly get a word in edgewise anyhow as the grownups, including Don and Lil, had all the main topics arranged step by step in their minds and had definite ideas as to how they wanted them carried through. Of course, Don and Lil were there acting the part of the anchor to keep your dad from getting too carried away, i.e., inviting all his patients to get back at them for inviting him to so many weddings.

January 17, 1961

I did ask Dad about the talk at the "4 Cs" restaurant. Here's how it proceeded. My dad got there first and was greeted by all four bosses, who congratulated him on soon becoming a father-in-law and then was escorted to the bar for a drink. Then your dad came and they began with a tour of the upstairs banquet hall (it's large enough!). Your dad was most satisfied with the setup. The manager said he would decorate and set it up any way we wanted, but he suggested putting in 23 long tables so that people could be served on all four sides and he said that they would try to arrange for whatever we need if it's within their power.

Now for the price. Dad was completely floored. Even as a special favor he didn't expect this but Paul estimated about $1.50 [$13.50 in 2021 dollars] per person. Dad said that we had wanted something a bit different from chow mein, etc. Even with fancier dishes Paul promised it wouldn't be more than $2.00. It's too unbelievable to be true that they could be so accommodating at the 4 Cs. For champagne, Dad felt that it would be only fair that the restaurant make some money on one item and offered to buy the liquor from them. But Paul told Dad to bring our own bottles and he'll serve them and they'll also provide the punch.

It seems that everything for the reception is in good hands and all that is left is for Alice and Mom to get together with Paul to plan the menu. So our dads left overjoyed and with full stomachs. The 4 Cs also treated them for lunch. Is it possible that people still do business this way?

January 17, 1961

Apparently the clan is completely Stanford directed so the invitations will be printed on red paper (in Chinese and English). This will also cut the cost as well as satisfy those who can't read English. As far as the place for the reception goes, the Four Seas seemed to be the most convenient place if we are married at Old St. Mary's. We'll also be following Mom and Dad's footsteps as they were married at Old St. Mary's and they had their traditional banquet at the old Hang Far Low, now the Four Seas.

January 18, 1961

I'm finding it hard to realize that our wedding plans are in their active stages. I will first attempt to get a guest list in order this weekend. And if there is time I would like to look at silver patterns.

January 22, 1961

I called up I. Magnin's to inquire about the arrival of their new bridal fashions, but they couldn't be shown until after their fashion show this Monday. So we altered our plans, window shopped a bit (the dresses were on window display) and looked at china and silver. I shocked Mom with our revolutionary china. Fortunately she is getting accustomed to it. But with the silver I had wanted to get as many things out of the way before the big rush of other things pile up and we don't have time. Cousin George will have the cake baked for us as he works for the Pisano Baking Company.

January 23, 1961

Today is the day I meet Mom for dinner after work and then to see the glorious wedding gowns. I purchased another bride's magazine this morning while waiting for the bus but haven't seen anything alluring. However, there was an interesting article that I'll send up to you. It's written by a Protestant minister who has some excellent comments on two people learning to live together. I am so anticipating the sight of what our wedding might possibly look like.

January 24, 1961
Now for the exciting account of last night's show. I met Mom for a quick dinner and we went to the dime store to pick up the file cards for our wedding list. Then we decided to get over to Magnin's early in order to secure a good seat. Even that was too late for a seat in the main room and we were shuffled off to a side anteroom. We were greeted by hostesses in pink bridesmaid dresses with huge baskets of sample perfume. The flowing dresses and picture hats[36] made them look as if they were flowers plucked right out of the garden. The first few bridal parties, including the mothers of the brides and grooms, came out in brilliant pink following the "pink champagne" theme.

I must interrupt the program to give this news flash: we have the church for July 9th! Mother and Auntie Marie finally tracked Father McGuire down this afternoon and procured the church as well straightened out many matters. Going to a priest that we know certainly saves much rigamarole. This afternoon he even located the church where I was baptized as I need my baptismal and confirmation papers to verify technically that I'm Catholic.

He further suggested that we not decorate the church too lavishly with flowers as that would detract from the

---

36 A fancy woman's hat with a wide brim.

218

beauty of the cathedral. The church doesn't have the carpet
runners for the aisle but they can be rented from the florist
on Powell Street.

Another technicality has been altered—hooray for
the Pope. Three years ago they finally lifted the ban on
non-Catholics being married at the altar. Previously
they had to stand in front of the communion rail. The
one inconvenience is that pictures can't be taken in the
church. They do have a beautiful courtyard, which provides
a lovely setting for pictures. Thanks to Mom and Father
McGuire, one more task is accomplished. Now it's our turn
to have the little talks with the good Father. I'll go see him
sometime next week and then call Father Tierney. I called
your dad after dinner. I could almost see him give a sigh of
relief that the date is now definitely settled.

Now back to the fashion show. Dress after dress came
out. There was the cutest little boy as ring bearer. But we
aren't having one in our service. As the last model left the
floor, we dashed across the street to the City of Paris to see
if we could catch the last glimpse of theirs. While crossing
the street we noticed hoards of mothers and daughters
carrying blue folders and yellow daffodils. As it turned
out, they were coming from the City of Paris show hoping
to catch the last of Magnin's. The City of Paris had racks
of bridal dresses, so in a matter of a few minutes we went
through the whole collection. Then a quick look over at
Macy's and finally home to bed.

January 25, 1961

There are many things one can do on the bus and I'm very
glad for that time. I can't begin to tell you how much nicer
it has been meeting Dad down in Chinatown (and driving

219

home with him) and the amount of wedding planning that can be done then.

Do you realize that six months of planning is only for a 15-minute show? But this is definitely the most thrilling thing of my entire life and I'm getting more excited by the day. I don't know how I can possibly last through the last month of work. Even now, I can't wait to leave the lab each night.

January 27, 1961
Mother had lunch at the 4 Cs yesterday as one of the owners was there and gave her the grand tour of the upstairs dining room. Mom is not certain that it will hold 600. I couldn't believe Dad. He thinks it would be nice to have for music at the reception—none other than the Kingston Trio. Dreamer, I said. That would turn our wedding more than ever into a circus. You can sigh a sigh of relief. We won't have to give a dance performance in front of all those googly-eyed people at our wedding. With 600 people there'll be no room for dancing. But after it all I do want to dance with you in private so keep up your practicing. Oh do I dread the thought of thank-you notes. How nice it would be if you would hire a secretary for me!

January 29, 1961
I took time off yesterday to talk further with my parents about the wedding. I made a huge list of items I would like as presents for Mom to suggest to people who wanted some ideas. I really couldn't think of very many specific items except of course MONEY! But then you really can't tell people that this is what we would appreciate most of all. However, Mom will probably hint that since we are

planning to live elsewhere and will do much moving, we would not be able to lug large items or fragile pieces.

Father spent the afternoon on the guest list. Starting from the end of the alphabet, he got to the Ls and used up 150 file cards. That multiplied by two brings us up to 300, n'est-ce pas?? I fear that we will have to go through quite a process of elimination! Then there is still the Cheu list and our own personal list to consider, but if we are highly selective we can still try to keep it down to 600.

Saturday belonged again to the series of our typical Saturdays. We didn't make it to the 10:00 a.m. wedding seminar so the day began with the fashion show at Saks Fifth Avenue. It was an elegant experience seeing the dress parade in their plush gown salon and then to be served coffee and danish pastry afterwards. I tried on my first bridal gown. It was so absolutely thrilling to be bundled in layer and layer of neat petticoats topped with lace and silk and trailed with a long cathedral train. I felt like a queen in all her grandeur as I glided into the salon to find all eyes turned in my direction as I looked in the great mirror for a complete view. The dress I tried on was quite beyond my means so we suspended our decision and went to lunch. After lunch with Grandma and aunties, we dashed over to the Emporium for their show. We had planned to do some trying on there but all the dresses were still stashed away for other fashion shows, so we went over to Magnin's to look at theirs. The bridal salon was so crowded that one couldn't even find a place to sit. After waiting for half an hour we gave up, made an appointment for next Saturday, and left downtown.

January 31, 1961

Last night was Grandma Lee's birthday and the Lee clan got together to give her a party at the Four Seas. That was the first time I've had a formal dinner there and I was thoroughly impressed with the food and atmosphere. I also met Paul Soong, who will take care of the reception. Your dad talked to him the other day and was told that they had cancelled a party of 52 tables because of our wedding day. Weren't we fortunate to have selected the date so early?

I am still poring over magazines in hopes of finding a silver pattern. I'm a bit concerned about what we should use as serving dishes with our china. The only thing that will possibly look good with it is silver. I can't imagine us getting that much silver service as gifts. The only solution I can think of is to dish all the food out in the kitchen. As young newlyweds, we probably wouldn't want to entertain quite as formally. Or did we decide that we do want to entertain "correctly"?

February 1, 1961

Never has Dad appeared more enthusiastic over an assigned task. He's finished the list for our side. He's been so concerned with the guest list that he's even gotten up in the middle of the night to work on it. Of course, there will no doubt be many minor changes but nevertheless, the basic structure is in order.

Being that I am tone deaf, you are the only possible candidate to select music for the church and reception. However, before you assume the assignment, you must promise not to have a vocalist singing merrily away during the ceremony. All right? As you are a musician yourself, the program is completely left to your aesthetic taste.

February 3, 1961

This weekend was one of a full and eventful schedule. I started Saturday morning at I. Magnin's and went through their bridal collection. There was nothing interesting in a reasonable price range. Then I met Diane L. for lunch (she was a music major but took quite a few biology courses and claims to know you). She's now an assistant buyer at Macy's. After lunch we rejoined Mom at the White House, where her friend is the bridal consultant. They were very sweet there but unfortunately they didn't have a single thing that was appropriate for a cathedral wedding. But the woman was going to wire to New York for a dress I saw in one of the magazines. We then went to the City of Paris, where the bridal salon was so packed. But since they had all the dresses on the rack we could survey the entire collection at a glance and didn't see what we wanted. We proceeded to Macy's and the dearest woman, an ex-nurse and now semi-retired but working part-time. She's one of those delightful women who is more interested in pleasing the prospective bride than making a big sale. We spent two hours there and were just about ready to call it a day when she brought out "The Dress." I put it on and Mom immediately jumped in glee! There and then we completed the transaction and made them put it in the vault so that no one else would see it. So another important project is completed. You are to be surprised so I can't even whisper a word about the dress to you, except that I feel so royal and elegant in it that I don't want to take it off. But there is so much dress and miles of train that I feel like a two-ton truck rolling down the street.

Sunday I had to pick up my parents for a wedding. It was a typical Chinatown wedding and we picked up ideas on what not to do. (They hadn't planned definitely on the receiving line so when that time came it was utter confusion and everyone forgot about it.) My parents are certainly making it a point not to miss a single wedding invitation. Even father is paying more attention.

February 7, 1961

I heard through the grapevine that you called home and rushed your dad to start on the list. At this point I'm very curious as to how many invites will be sent out. I only hope that our guests will not bring their entire clan of children. Gosh, at the wedding Sunday the place was packed with screaming little kids and it resembled a circus instead of a solemn wedding.

Since I've registered our date and choice of china at the downtown stores I've been swamped with circulars about wedding invites and calls from photo studios who want our business. So I've given them the story that you have taken care of arranging for a photographer.

It's very amusing when shopping at the bridal salons to see the same prospective brides each week. After a while I begin to expect to see the same faces everywhere I go.

Mother truly had a wonderful visit with Alice at lunch and she particularly appreciates the opportunity to know Alice better. And don't you agree that understanding brings happy relations, especially when it comes to in-laws? It makes it much easier for us, anyway.

February 13, 1961

You were the person who wanted the "red and white" wedding and I was just trying to please you. According to the bridal consultant, red is a popular color for summer weddings in San Francisco. But so as not to shock all our guests and completely blind them, we could be more subdued and use light rose or coral. I also will have to talk to the manufacturer to see if he'll make the dresses in a cheaper fabric and bring the cost from $80 [$720 in 2021 dollars] to $50 [$450 in 2021 dollars]. I'll allow you a preview of the bridesmaid dresses to divert your curiosity from mine. It's quite different from the run-of-the-mill bridesmaid dresses—no frills and ruffles so that they can be worn as cocktail dresses. In fact, it was copied from one of Magnin's exclusive cocktail dresses.

February 13, 1961

My parents and I went to another wedding to make acute observations. This one was at a Methodist church in Stonestown, where one escapes the frantic Chinatown atmosphere. It was a smaller wedding, but at that scale it was beautifully executed. I was particularly amazed at how smoothly everything went. The lines weren't long and crowded and there were chairs all through the hall for the guests to sit and talk. Very comfortable and the chow mein was delicious!

February 15, 1961

I've been thinking, do you suppose that I could still have a wedding ring made to my own specifications? The ring that goes with the engagement ring is really very unesthetic. It occurred to me yesterday that a wider band might be nice with one side the same height as the engagement ring, but then sloping down until it's the same height all around. Oh, I can't draw it right but maybe can describe it when you get back.

February 17, 1961

Another girl in the lab just got married two weeks ago and brought her wedding pictures. She had a beautiful medium-size wedding but you could tell from the pictures that calmness and serenity prevailed. But I wonder how she possibly stood up under finals the day before, wedding rehearsal, guests arriving from 1:30 a.m. up at 6:00 a.m., hair dresser, bridal breakfast, nuptial mass at 11:00 a.m. (both Catholics), and reception at 4:00 p.m..

That situation I don't want. However, Mother has been working on getting me to relax on our wedding day. Her first plan is to pick a hideaway, lock me up, and put me to sleep the night before and on the wedding day stuff me with shark fin soup. Yes, and a messenger will knock on your door and then you will have to gulp down soup whether or not you want it. It's Mom's cure-all.

February 20, 1961

Mother and I still can't decide on the color of the dresses for the bridesmaids. We've exhausted every color chart at Magnin's. First, I fell madly for "gold dust" and after 30 minutes finally convinced Mom that this would be the greatest effect, glistening in the candlelight of St. Mary's Cathedral. Mom became very enthusiastic and we put in the order for five dresses. As we were leaving it occurred to me that two of the bridesmaids might look completely washed out and ghastly in contrast with the brilliance of gold. So we returned to the salon and cancelled the order to debate some more. This may appear to be just a minor detail to you men, but a color can turn the ceremony from a solemn, beautiful occasion to literally a great circus. Can you think of anything worse happening?

February 21, 1961

You are full of good advice, especially about "Happy Time Wedding Day." We simply must set our minds to enjoy July 9th and not let it be a day of tension and pressure. We must sit down when you are back and spend days upon days organizing and organizing and making up instruction cards for everyone involved.

February 26, 1961

I have two more correspondences to take care of, including one to Cousin Izzie asking her to be a bridesmaid. Have you asked Mike yet? No. That can wait until you have more time after your orals.

March 1, 1961

By the end of this month, we should be well on our way with our wedding plans. I haven't felt in the mood for planning a scheme of things for the household etc. when you are not here with your ideas. Probably the first item on the agenda when you return will be invitations (your father hasn't completed his list so it must be growing longer and longer) as there are only April, May, and June left and invites should be sent out by June 20th. Then comes lots of shopping, so don't throw away your walking shoes. If I were in school I would be a lost cause. And in a way, I feel somewhat guilty that I distracted you in your studies.

Mother has been spending long hours giving me the indoctrination program on how to make my man be a happy husband.

Finally we are wed!

Chinese World, billed as "America's only bilingual Chinese-English daily newspaper, ran this announcement of our wedding on Thursday, July 27, 1961:

1,000 Guests At Young-Cheu Rites in Old St. Mary's Church

Over one thousand guests attended the wedding of Janey M. Young and Richard Alden Cheu in Old St. Mary's Church. Father John F. Tierney officiated at the single ring ceremony. The nuptial rites united two families with Stanford University backgrounds. Lt. Col. John C. Young, USAR, a Stanford graduate, escorted his daughter down the aisle. The bride graduated from the same university last year. The groom and his father, Dr. Henry D. F. Cheu, a San Francisco physician, are also Stanford graduates.

The bride wore a Princess Ling Bianca gown of candelite silk taffeta with a chapel train composed of three panels appliqued with French rose-point lace, re-embroidered with seed pearls and iridescent sequins. The crown was made of seed pearls and crystals with an elbow length silk illusion veil....

The reception was at the Four Seas Restaurant....

The newlyweds will reside in Portland, Oregon where the benedict, who received an M.A. at the University of Oregon, plans to work for his Ph.D. in physiology.

The bride is a microbiologist with the California Department of Public Health.

13. The Last Letter I Read to Janey

In a letter written on September 24, 1960, Janey wrote, "*In spite of my ripe old age of 22 years, I've still not seen snow fall. Is there a possibility that we might go up to Oregon to see the snow?*"

When we were graduate students at the University of Oregon medical school, from our kitchen window we had a view of snow-capped Mt. Hood, which we visited one very snowy and icy day. When we lived in Chicago, when I was studying for my MBA at Northwestern, Janey saw more snow than she wanted in the Blizzard of 1967, which dropped 23 inches of snow on the city—a record that still stands. We lived in Minneapolis during the winter of 1969, when the highest temperature in January was minus ten degrees. The local middle school converted its outdoor sports facility into an evening ice skating rink for the neighborhood. We took the children skating almost nightly. During our brief stint in Minneapolis, Janey talked about her desire to learn how to ski.

Our next move brought us to New Jersey and I started my new job as marketing manager for a New York City advertising agency that handled the Head Skis account. That created an opportunity for Janey and our three boys to learn to ski. Head Skis lent us adult skis and she borrowed a neighbor's children's skis. At every opportunity she took the children skiing. The youngest was so small that she placed him between her legs as they went up the hill on a rope tow. To help the boys learn how to get on and off a rope tow lift, I set up a rope tow inside the house and I was the motor. Janey quickly became an adept and fast skier on the intermediate trails. The culmination of our ski adventures was a family ski trip to Austria. We stopped skiing when the two older boys joined the high school fencing team and were told they could not do a winter sport that might injure their legs.

Janey was a member of the AT&T Bell Laboratories delegation that attended United Nations sessions in Geneva, Switzerland, two or more times a year. Her team negotiated the standards by which different national telephone systems connected with each other. Her signaling group explained their work by saying, "We're the ding-a-ling part of a telephone call." On one trip to Geneva, Janey introduced a few of her colleagues to skiing at the ski resort in Chamonix and realized how much she missed skiing. I mentioned her desire to ski again to my colleagues at Brookdale Community College in Middletown Township, New Jersey, where I was an adjunct professor teaching human physiology. One professor said, "You're an EMT. Ski areas use EMTs as ski patrollers." With some difficulty, since I didn't know how to ski, I managed to join a ski patrol at a ski area in upstate New York where they wanted my emergency medical skills and said they would teach me to ski. As a family member of a ski patroller, Janey skied for free while I was on duty each weekend.

Janey greatly enjoyed skiing and was very skilled. In 2003, when she was 65 years old, I noticed that she was having difficulties making right turns while skiing. She grudgingly allowed me to do a neurological and physical examination of her and I concluded she had a neurological problem. She was eventually diagnosed with a terminal brain disease with an average life expectancy of seven years. Over the next several years, we traveled to destinations she wanted to visit while she was still ambulatory. When Hurricane Sandy slammed into New York City on October 22, 2012, we were on the Queen Elizabeth 2 returning from London, where Janey wanted to see the Crown Jewels. She was hospitalized for a short while and then came home, where I had set up an intensive care unit in the apartment and hired a live-in nursing assistant to provide weekday daytime care. From this point on, Janey was bedridden.

Each night I prepared her for sleep with the following routine: a facial massage with a skin cream from Germany to care for her chapped skin and to provide a human touch, reading one of her letters out loud in sequence, saying a nightly prayer, and singing her favorite hymn to her, *Tantum Ergo*, in Latin. This routine continued nightly for nearly three years. By mid-May 2015, it was clear that she was clinically dying. Her vital signs were deteriorating, she was no longer eating, was having difficulty swallowing, and had lapsed into a coma. Despite her condition, I continued the nightly routine and read her letter of March 7, 1961, in which she wrote:

> I was terribly amused by the tales of the woes and problems of a young bride (another lab technician). What a mad whirl, and I think that I go at top speed now. In spite of it all, I can't wait. I still maintain that one should never iron when there are so many other things that have to be done, like thank-you notes. This girl gets seven written each day and she's one of these faster writers compared to me. Her weeks sound very much like our days of entertaining down in Palo Alto and rushing up to San Francisco for other appointments. It may be good if we lived away from that hectic life of social obligations. But whatever, we'll have fun and love.

At that moment, Janey awoke from her coma, opened her eyes, and said to me, "Let's elope!" I was so shocked that all I could say was, "We can't do that. Our parents would be so upset. Your best friend eloped and her husband's family never accepted her." Janey replied, "Oh, okay." She paused and then said, "I love you" and slipped back into a coma. For the next day or so, I watched her continuing efforts to resist dying. Finally, I whispered in her ear, "It's time for you to go home to God. You know I have work to do, a history book to write, and I'll be okay." She relaxed and died peacefully a few hours later.

Music was an important channel of communication between us that didn't require words. I've added the lyrics of this song, from the musical *Carousel* by Rodgers and Hammerstein, as a final song for us.

"You'll Never Walk Alone"

When you walk through a storm
Hold your head up high
And don't be afraid of the dark

At the end of a storm
There's a golden sky
And the sweet silver song of a lark

Walk on through the wind
Walk on through the rain
Though your dreams be tossed and blown

Walk on, walk on
With hope in your heart
And you'll never walk alone
You'll never walk alone
Walk on, walk on
With hope in your heart
And you'll never walk alone

You'll never walk alone

Part 3

Janey's Yin and Yang Personality

Janey's Name

Janey's Chinese name,[37] 梅芳 [Mui Fong], means "peach blossom." It is a name that captures the essence of love in a very symbolic way, especially in Chinese culture. Peaches are native to China and date back as far as 6,000 B.C. In ancient China, peaches were a symbol of love, unity, luck, immortality, longevity, prosperity, good health, perpetual vitality, and all things good. Peach tree blossom season is the best season for young couples to wed and Chinese brides carry peach blossoms in the wedding ceremony. Peaches are often depicted in Chinese paintings, sculptures, pottery, clothing, and even in food shaped to look like a peach. A Chinese folktale tells the story of a poet and scholar of the Tang Dynasty named Cui Hu who searched for a girl he had fallen in love with and was able to find her again thanks to the peach tree in her yard. Thus the peach blossom came to symbolize love. In the contemporary world, peach blossoms are commonly purchased during Chinese New Year, which is close to Valentine's Day on the Gregorian calendar, to symbolize love and prosperity in the coming year. It is thought that the more buds that bloom, the more love there is to come in the new year. The motif of peaches reflects Janey's personality throughout her life as she strove to break barriers, showing the power of her love, resilience, and perseverance.

---

37 Thank you to Kimberly Szeto for this information.

The ancient Chinese philosophical concept of yin and yang has been known since as long ago as 300 BC. It states that all things in nature exist as opposing pairs, including human personality traits, which are traditionally described as female (yin) and male (yang) characteristics. Examples are presented in the following chart.

YIN	YANG
Female	Male
Earth	Heaven
Passive	Active
Duality	Monality
Water	Fire (creativity)
Quiescence	Vigor
Soft	Strong
Moon (weakness)	Sun (strength)
Poor	Rich

The yin and yang symbol, below, represents the complementary nature of yin and yang and the dots indicate a small amount of the opposing element within yin and yang.

Philosophers from Aristotle to Kant and others from the Enlightenment to contemporary times have emphasized that the highest goal of human achievement is a life governed by rationality and that man is more rational than woman. Therefore, man occupies a dominant position over woman.

Contemporary philosopher Michael Slote argues in his book, *From Enlightenment to Receptivity: Rethinking Our Values*, that overemphasis on rationality has failed to recognize the complementary aspect of receptivity that provides balance to rationality. He states that every personality trait, in men and women, has features of both receptivity and rationality. Yin focuses on receptivity, a capacity to be "receptive to the needs and aspirations of others, to what we can learn from those we disagree with, to the natural world around us, and to what our own lives have brought us or may bring us in the future."[38] Yang represents the traditional rational aspects of personality traits that are usually ascribed to men only.

According to Slote, receptivity acknowledges the roles of emotions, empathy, caring, and morality in shaping human behavior. Being irrational at times can be beneficial, as in the case of love. Slote writes,

> When we love, we can't be entirely objective either about the merits or about the beliefs/attitudes of the person we love. We will be partial to the person's opinions/attitudes compared … to those we know less well. It seems that perfect or thoroughgoing objectivity is something we cannot achieve unless our lives are starved of significant relationships.[39]

From Slote's perspective, a "good life" can be achieved by allowing the receptiveness and rationality of one's personality traits to be expressed appropriately.

Traditionally, an inclination to adventure has been considered a male characteristic while a preference for security has been seen as a female characteristic. Slote refers to contemporary feminism's position, that "adventure and adventurousness" are as important to women as they may be to men and security and prudence are as relevant to men

38 Michael Slote, *From Enlightenment to Receptivity: Rethinking Our Values* (Oxford: Oxford University Press, 2013), p. x.
39 Slote, p. 83.

as they are for women. Slote is simply stating a fact of life, which argues against assigning gender roles to these traits.

In several of her letters, Janey expresses her desire for a life of adventure as well as the importance of a financially secure married life. However, her most distinctive personality traits included an intense need for privacy, an intuitive sense of higher mathematics, an emphasis on precision, and an acute palate she used in preparing foods. In St. Louis our neighbors were also young families and frequently the mothers of the wives asked Janey to give their daughters cooking lessons. These traits interacted and expressed themselves in different ways depending on the situation. A few examples will illustrate what I mean.

For about seven years, I was the co-director of a seminar for Asian American managers on "How to be a good manager and not lose your culture." We conducted three-day seminars for clients across the United States, including McDonald's, AT&T, federal agencies, and others. My partner was a human resources specialist and every seminar participant was required to complete the Myers-Briggs personality test. One summer Sunday, I was scheduled to go to Washington, D.C., to meet my consulting partner and conduct a seminar. Weekend traffic on the New Jersey Turnpike was congested and I had to quickly maneuver my way through traffic to not miss my train. Janey's only comment during the hour's drive was, "You're driving like a fireman." I arrived at the train station shortly before it arrived. Once onboard, I called Janey and said, "I made it with five minutes to spare." When I arrived in Washington, I called her again and said, "I made the train with ten minutes to spare." She replied, "Why are you lying to me? Was it five minutes or ten?" I thought about that exchange during the seminar and realized that we were delivering completely different messages to each other. My words were meant to imply "approximately" and Janey was demanding precision. She received her doctorate in education and psychology and I reasoned that she must have taken the Myers-Briggs test at some time in her studies. When I got home, I asked her what her Myers-Briggs score was. When I compared our scores, I truly understood her and our relationship for the first time. Her score indicated an "extreme introvert" personality, which explained her intense need for privacy, her unwillingness to speak until she was completely confident about what to say—especially in public—and her focus on precision.

On another occasion, Janey's math skills and precision were on display. I had managed to avoid taking calculus in high school and college. This caught up with me during my graduate studies and I was required to take a course in calculus at a local college in addition to my coursework at the medical school. I was sitting at a desk at home struggling to solve the assigned calculus problems when Janey walked by. She glanced down at the problem I was working on, calculated the answer in her head, and told me the answer to the first decimal point. Then she gave me the answer to the next problem with no greater effort than breathing before walking away.

Another episode involved our interest in California wines that we developed together during our courtship. Shortly after arriving in Portland to begin our graduate studies, we went for a stroll through the downtown area and came across an unusual window display of bottles of wine cradled in red velvet—not something we San Francisco snobs had expected to see in Portland, Oregon. The store was not a wine shop but a company that constructed advertising displays. When we stepped into the store, we were met by a white-haired gentleman named Bert Harris with the personality of Johnny Kan and a flair reflecting his involvement with the theatrical world. He had a passion for fine wines and was beside himself with joy that a young couple, knowledgeable in fine wines, had suddenly appeared at his multipurpose shop. He taught a weekly evening course in wine in the back of the shop and sold wines to the attendees. He invited me to be his volunteer assistant, opening and pouring up to ten wines a session. It was a mutually beneficial relationship. He got an assistant knowledgeable about wines and I gained first-hand knowledge of wines that I only knew from reading about them. At the class's annual wine dinner, I was the sommelier and Janey attended free of charge. He virtually adopted us as his niece and nephew and included us in various family events. We celebrated one of Janey's birthdays with Bert Harris at one of Portland's finest restaurants. During dinner, I happened to mention Janey's acute palate and that she could identify different brands of cognac. She, of course, demurred. Bert went to the bar, had the bartender pour four different cognacs into four numbered sniffers, and brought them to our table. Without giving Janey an opportunity to clear her palate, he asked her to name the brands. She correctly identified three of the four. It should be noted that no one had given us any cognac as a wedding present.

Janey's great passion was cooking, which she used to express love and friendship. Her mother was an excellent cook and Janey received informal but critical lessons from the head chef at Ming's Restaurant, located near the Stanford campus. Janey's father was also an investor in Ming's. At the time there were no Chinese grocery stores near Palo Alto and Janey would drop by Ming's for handouts of Chinese spices and ingredients. At the restaurant, she learned from the chef to use her hands to measure the amount of different ingredients and sense the correct cooking temperature and timing without using a thermometer or timer. She insisted on privacy in the kitchen so she could totally focus on cooking. When I was at General Mills developing new products, she was invited to test a new Chinese sauce in the test kitchens. There were different setups for different types of cooking: gas, electric, stovetop, and so on. At each setup, Janey tested the sauce with different foods while being watched by the test kitchen supervisor and a home economist taking notes. It was a situation that suited her personality: privacy, focus, and precision.

The kitchens in our Fair Haven, New Jersey, and New York City homes were designed to keep people out of Janey's cooking area.

They could watch her but not enter her turf. That was also one reason she enjoyed sailing: no one was allowed in the galley while she was cooking. She disliked steering the vessel and other sailing chores and only did those under protest.

Privacy for concentration and mathematics were key factors in a political fundraising dinner we hosted in our New Jersey home for 40 people. I asked her, "How will you be able to cook for 40 people? "Simple," she answered. "Just do the math." She said no more as she expected me to take care of all the noncooking details. When the guests had arrived and were seated, Janey began cooking. The volunteer servers waited patiently outside the cooking area, watching with amazement. Each dish, portioned for 40 people, was served in proper sequence to the guests, at the correct temperature and properly seasoned. Privacy, focus, math, and precision were the skills she drew on to achieve what seemed remarkable to everyone except Janey.

The Energy Activation Concept and Janey

The energy activation concept is taught in every basic high school and chemistry course. This fundamental principle says that a minimum amount of energy is needed to start a chemical reaction. Behavior is the result of a chemical reaction between nerve cells. Nerve cells "talk to each other" when one nerve cell sends a chemical messenger to another nerve cell, which causes the receiving cell to respond. Broadly speaking, a minimum amount of energy is required to initiate brain cell activity and behavior. This was particularly true for Janey as she traveled along her career path.

The first instance when Janey needed additional energy (prodding) to overcome her introverted lack of self-confidence was the day before classes began for the 1961 fall semester at the University of Oregon medical school. We rented a one-bedroom apartment a few blocks from school in the mountain-top community that contained the medical and nursing schools, the Veterans Administration hospital, a grocery store, and a Catholic chapel. We were literally in a forest where trees were being logged. (A 19th-century entrepreneur tried to corner the Portland transportation rail hub by the Willamette River. Lacking a topographical map, he bought a mountain, which he eventually donated to the state, which situated the medical complex there.) The night before classes began and I would register for my physiology fellowship, we had a serious discussion about what Janey was going to do. On the one hand, she wanted to do what her parents—and society—expected of her: get a job as a laboratory technician and support her husband during his graduate school years. On the other hand, she wanted to have a career, as she had said in her letters.

I will admit to taking advantage of her in our discussion to get my way. Whenever Janey wanted to overcome her father's resistance to something she wanted to do, she would sit on his lap to talk with him. So I used reverse psychology. I had her sit on my lap, and said to her, "You are completely qualified to get a fellowship. You know more about immunology than any of the microbiology faculty members. You're smarter than I am. If I can get a fellowship, you can too!" The next day at dinner, she told me that the Microbiology Department had accepted her as a doctoral student and gleefully said, "My fellowship is bigger than yours."

After leaving Portland, we lived in Chicago for two years while I studied for my MBA at Northwestern University's Kellogg Graduate School of Management. I attended classes during the day and worked as a night shift cashier, while doing my homework, from 6:00 p.m. to midnight at the Trader Vic's restaurant in Palmer House. Our third child was born shortly after we arrived in Chicago and Janey had her hands full caring for three children under the age of six while managing our household located in, according to an article in a

Chicago newspaper, the poorest neighborhood in the city. One night a week she and her best friend attended an art course where she sculpted.

A requirement for completing the MBA program was attendance at the graduation ceremony. I received a dispensation from attendance because we had just enough money to pay for gas for the trip from Chicago to a marketing position with a new Monsanto venture in St. Louis. Monsanto was aware of our dire poverty and had a check waiting for me when I arrived. After depositing the check in a local bank, we rented a three-story townhouse in a community complex close enough to Monsanto for me to ride a bicycle (on a freeway) to and from work. We went from dire poverty to a wonderful lifestyle in a matter of hours. The communal pool was next to our apartment. Janey and the boys spent many hours swimming and relaxing at the pool during the summer. A few months after we arrived in St. Louis, I walked by a bulletin board at Monsanto and saw a particularly interesting help wanted notice. A local Catholic high school needed a biology teacher. I called the high school and told them that Janey was available for the position and they accepted her over the telephone. After work, I went home and told Janey that she would be teaching high school biology beginning next week and she should arrange for a babysitter to care for the children. She didn't argue and agreed.

Janey was more than qualified to teach basic high school biology. I was a biology teaching assistant at Stanford and Oregon and could help her whenever she came across an unfamiliar topic. For example, one morning she said she had to do a frog dissection demonstration and didn't know how to do it. She managed to avoid taking the basic biology series at Stanford, which included examining plants and animals. "No problem," I said. I went out to the pool, grabbed a frog that made the mistake of jumping into the suburban pool, and came back in. I showed Janey how to kill the frog by hitting the back of its head against the edge of the breakfast table and then proceeded to dissect it on a place mat. The children were simultaneously shocked and fascinated. Maybe that's why none of them became biologists or doctors. From my perspective, teaching biology would help Janey regain her mental footing as a researcher after the two-year pause in Chicago and prepare her for the next unknown step along her career path. Janey taught for only one year before we moved to Minneapolis for my new job at General Mills. She and the school principal, a nun, became friends and they stayed in contact for many years. What she could not anticipate was that her year of high school teaching positioned her for teaching advanced technology to scientists at AT&T's Bell Laboratories.

Janey and the boys were in Minneapolis for only one year. Again, she had her hands full raising the children and managing the household. I left Minneapolis after six months, leaving Janey and the children to finish the school year, to take up a marketing position with the New York advertising agency that provided advertising and public relations for the new Monsanto venture I had worked on. It took six months for the agency to find me at General Mills and offer me a marketing position in New York, which I accepted. We moved from Minneapolis to New Jersey and purchased a three-bedroom Levitt-constructed home in Somerset, a suburban commuter community close to Rutgers University's New Brunswick campus, where Janey resumed her career.

The most monumental and demanding energy of activation episode occurred after Janey completed her doctorate at Rutgers. She applied for a position with AT&T's Bell Laboratories. She came home and said she failed her interview. An intense three-hour argument ensued. I tried to convince her to call the interviewer and ask for a second interview. She refused. I cajoled and argued until she agreed to call the next morning and request a second interview. She had two problems: she didn't want to try again something she had failed, and she didn't know what to say to the interviewer. She finally agreed to say what I wrote down for her: "Hello, Joan. This is Janey. I would like to have another interview." Bell Laboratories motto was "We hire only the best and brightest" and they were used to working with technical people like Janey. Her request for another interview was granted.

AT&T Bell Laboratories

Janey's second interview at Bell Labs included meetings with several members of the technical staff. They learned that she had an extensive record of independent research beginning in her undergraduate years at Stanford under the mentorship of Gus Nossal, Av Mitchison, and Ollie Makela. In her graduate studies at the University of Oregon Medical School, her research focused on transplantation genetics. She earned an MEd at Rutgers in 1972 soon after we moved to New Jersey from Minneapolis. She was the associate director at the Institute for Science, Technology, and Social Science Education at the Rutgers Center for Coastal and Environmental Studies from 1976 to 1981. During her tenure at the institute, she published seven papers. While working full-time there she was also a doctoral student. She received a doctorate in psychology and education in 1982 at Rutgers. Her doctoral dissertation topic was "The Organization of Visual Information in a Part-Whole Figure Synthesis Task: Strategies and Task Conditions."

In addition to working and studying for her doctorate, Janey was a mother of three high school students and the wife of a firefighter/EMT and marketing consultant, managed our household, and frequently entertained colleagues and friends at dinner parties in our home—she cooked, of course. She often complained to me, "The guests are having too good a time talking with each other at our candlelit dinners and don't want to go home." She found time to be actively involved in several Fair Haven organizations, including the Arts Council and the Sailing Club Board of Directors, and she was appointed to the Environmental Council by the mayor. She needed the evening glass of wine at the end of each day to unwind as we caught up on each other's activities and news.

During the series of job interviews at Bell Labs, Janey learned about the organization of the staff along a hierarchy arranged according to their educational qualifications. According to Jerry Rubin, a former scientist at the Labs,

> The Research Department (Area 10) was managed by a Vice President who supervised Areas managed by Directors. The Directors in turn managed Departments. The Departments were led by Department Heads who had staffs consisting of MTSs, (Members of the Technical Staff—PHD's); AMTSs, (Associate Member of the Technical Staff—Master's Degree); STAs (Senior Technical Aides—Bachelors Degree) and TAs (Technical Aides). The vast majority of staff consisted of exceptional scientists with PhD Degrees.[40]

Hanna Alger worked at Bell Labs until her retirement in 1989. I asked her how women were treated at Bell Labs when she worked there. She told me,

> In general, they were a step below [men]. It had been a culture until about 1965—like in the airlines, they would be mail girls or stewardesses. They expected to meet people who could provide for them well. They were attractive, talented. They hired educated kinds of people, but if you missed college you could come to Bell Labs and you would have the same kind of chance meeting the same kind of people providing the same kind of environment.

---

40 Posted at Quora.com, https://www.quora.com/When-did-Bell-Labs-add-the-Distinguished-Member-of-Technical-Staff-title

So the women who were there before were these attractive women who were kind of available as potential spouses. Then they got a few people, like Mary O'D., who was a physicist. They had three women who were really scientists. But Mary was never really accepted in the core. She was OK, she was technical, but she stayed at the bottom. That was the way Bell Labs was when I came in.

Then we had a group, really when programming became the big thing, then they got people who started out as coders, and a lot of them were women. That brought in a large number of women and I think I was considered a part of that group. There were not many of us [women] who popped out of that. I went to grad school in '65, and I don't remember how many of us from Bell Labs went. All of the men were promoted and I was not.[41]

In December 1983, Janey was hired as a member of the technical Staff because she had her doctorate. She told me she taught Advanced Technology to the technical staff. However, her 1990 Bell Labs internal résumé revealed that she did more than teach the technical staff. It described her position and work in these words:

Instructional designer in Systems Training Center: Assessed and critiqued the course development and production procedures and organizations of the center. Translated the recommendations by working with course developers, software developers, and the production and editorial staff to establish an integrated course development system. The system published in "Instructional Quality Planning and Methods" was implemented across the center and now has been incorporated in the "Uniform Course Development

41 Interview with Terry Alger, July 8, 2021.

Methodology" currently used by the Kelly Education and Training Center.

Not long afterward, Janey began working on a project with an international scope with multiple roles. Her primary role was described in this way:

> Project Coordinator and instructional designer for the Information Communication Institute of Singapore (ICIS) project, a joint collaboration between AT&T and the National Computer Board of Singapore. This was the highest priority project for the Kelly Education and Training Center in 1989 and involved over 75 persons in the development of 18 courses and a practicum for an intensive, year-long training program in telecommunications software development.

Janey's work on this project involved seven different roles, such as "formulated, wrote, and implemented the standards and procedures for the development and production of the courses," serving on the task force to manage and maintain over 22,000 pages of documentation, and designing and delivering workshops that accommodated over 100 AT&T managers.

Distinguished Member Technical Staff Award

According to Stanley Lippman, a former programmer at Bell Labs, the Distinguished Member Technical Staff (DMTS) award "was an attempt to rectify the career pathway paradox that exists in technology. That is, an engineer is both a professional and a person, and at some point in one's career, in order to break a certain level of salary, prestige, and influence, one was expected to move from a technology track to the management track; otherwise, one's career was viewed as a dead-end at some point."[42] The first group of technical staff members to receive the DMTS, established in 1982, included two men and two women. Terry Alger and Janey Cheu were the two women.

Janey was one of thousands of MTSs at Bell Labs. Virtually all of them had worked at the Labs for years, if not decades. Janey was one of very few Asian American women MTSs. How was it that Janey, after only three years at Bell Labs, was singled out to be in the first group of four MTSs to receive the DMTS award? According to Hanna Alger,

Janey received her [DMTS] truly due to competently doing telephone kind of work. When she was on the standards committee for international standards for telecommunications, Janey did a marvelous job. More than an adequate job, she really made a valuable contribution. Her PhD topic was applicable to that actual work. She must have come to Bell Labs just before her dissertation was published. I can remember in my first conversation about that—and she wasn't selling herself—we were discussing with interest on the topic and it was something I had never thought about before.

After 1965, work was recognized. Advancement was not going to happen often. Susan Strauss was one of the exceptions. We had worked together before Susan was promoted. We had worked on a government contract, the Nike missile contract. She was one of the three people assembling the [massive] document. . . . She had managed to get it assembled and the government accepted it. The government had probably decided beforehand they were going to do it—just submit the document. Then she was

42 Quora.com, https://www.quora.com/When-did-Bell-Labs-add-the-Distinguished-Member-of-Technical-Staff-title

promoted to supervisor but never got any further than that. But then they used her for teaching, organizing, not for really research. But Susan herself was very interested in women's rights. ... She was interested in feminist rights.

Susan Strauss was Janey's supervisor. It was Susan who brought attention to Janey's work and worked tirelessly advocating for her and mentoring her. Janey would come home and complain that "Susan keeps pushing me to speak up and let people know what I do." Ultimately, it was Janey's utilization of her unique combination of personality traits, research skills, and doctoral dissertation that resulted in the successful accomplishment of the most important project of the Kelly Education and Training Center at that time. But it was Susan who lifted Janey to the highest level of technical recognition at Bell Labs.

A Long-Distance Conversation Without Words or Images

Merriam-Webster's definition of *conversation* is "an oral exchange of sentiments, observations, opinions, or ideas." Janey said she disliked taking telephone calls while she was at work because they interfered with her concentration. She preferred speaking with her colleagues in person, probably because their conversations were technical and detailed. The culture in her group at Bell Labs was very collegial, she said—"You go see the person you want to talk with." This made a lot of sense because more than half of the information in a face-to-face conversation is communicated through body language. I only called her at work if it was an essential call. As a consultant, I used the telephone as needed to make business calls but spent much of my time traveling to meet with clients.

At home, however, after-work conversation was the glue that held our marriage together. Whenever we were both at home, we would sit down at the end of the day when the children were asleep and the house was quiet, and we would have a glass of wine. We chatted about anything that came to mind. We didn't really discuss each others' work in detail, but we were aware of each other's projects. If during the course of our own work I came across some information or an article that might be of interest to Janey, I would share it with her during our late-night cocktail hour. And she did the same for me. If one or the other was traveling domestically, whoever was on the road would call home in the evening for a brief catch-up call. It was difficult to call home when one of us was traveling internationally because of time zone differences and hectic work schedules. For example, the flight from New Jersey to Taiwan included a layover in Tokyo, a 24-hour flight in total. Within an hour of my landing in Taipei, the client expected to meet with me. Other than for interruptions due to travel, the late-evening chat was a perpetual habit that persisted throughout our five-decade marriage.

On one occasion, Janey had been on a trip to Atlanta and returned the same day I left on a trip. Between her arrival at home and my departure earlier in the day, there was a sudden and violent wind storm in the local area, perhaps a mini tornado. When I spoke to her that evening, I asked how things were. She said casually, "Oh, the wind storm must have been very strong. It knocked down a very old, tall tree two houses from us. It crushed our neighbor's garage, landed on our roof, and punched a hole in it. But there's nothing to worry about. The guys from your volunteer fire department had already tarped the roof before I arrived home. Our neighbor has arranged for a tree company to come with a crane to lift the tree off the roof and to repair the roof. Our neighbors are gathering tomorrow morning in our next door neighbor's yard for brunch and to watch the removal of the tree."

One day in the latter part of her career at Bell Labs, Janey came home one day and said that the education budget was being cut. She spent the next six months teaching herself electrical engineering and then applied for an engineering position in the signaling group, which she got. Two or three times a year, she and a group of engineers, accompanied by a U.S. State Department staff member, attended a United Nations session in Geneva, Switzerland, to negotiate signaling standards with national telephone companies from around the world. On the evening of her return home, I would wait for the limousine to pull into our circular driveway. I could hear the crunch of the tires on the gravel and I would go out to meet the car and Janey and bring in her luggage. Then we would have something to eat, have a glass of wine or two, and chat.

On one trip before the advent of cell phones, she was extremely late returning home from JFK Airport. Everything was ready for her return, including the usual vase of gladiolas in the foyer. I was really getting bored waiting, so I decided to pretend I was the butler. I put on my tuxedo and waited for the limousine to arrive. Knowing nothing about my plan to act as a butler, when Janey was about 20 miles from home, she told the driver, "My butler will come out and get the luggage." When the limousine pulled into the driveway, I went out to the car and the driver lowered his window and said, "The luggage is in the trunk." As I passed by Janey's window to get the luggage, I could see she was shocked to see me in a tuxedo. She quickly got out of the car and dashed into the house, pursing her lips to keep from laughing. I followed her in and we made sure the limousine was gone before we fell into each other's arms, laughing hysterically. We had never previously mentioned my pretending to be her butler on her return from Geneva—this was a pure coincidence.

Did we have an extrasensory experience? I leave it to you, the reader, to decide.

Part 4

Memorable Moments:
Oral History Interview with Janey

Below is a transcript of an interview I did with Janey at StoryCorps in New York City on June 30, 2011. StoryCorps is a nonprofit organization that began recording people's stories in a studio at New York's Grand Central Terminal in 2003. By 2011, when I recorded Janey's interview, StoryCorps had two studios in New York and studios in other U.S. cities. Interviews were conducted by an interviewer provided by Story Corps, except for Janey's interview, which I conducted. Each interviewee received an audio copy and printed transcript of the interview at no charge. Interviews are now recorded online. According to StoryCorps, it has recorded interviews with about 500,000 people across the United States since 2003. Some of the interviews are archived at the Library of Congress.

The Interview Transcript

My name is Richard Cheu and I'm 74 years old as of two weeks ago. Today's date is July 30, 2011, and we are in Foley Park in New York City. My relationship to my [StoryCorps] partner is that she is my wife.

My name is Janey Cheu and my age is 72. Today's date is July 30, 2011. We're located in Foley Park, and my relationship to you is that I am your wife.

Richard: Thank you. Janey, you have a very interesting background. You are part of that very small group of people known as American-

born Chinese born before World War II. What was it like to grow up and where did you grow up?

Janey: I was born in Los Angeles, California, and grew up in Whittier, California. I remember my early memories very well. Let's see . . .

What was Whittier like when you were growing up? You were born in 1938.

Whittier was a one-horse town. There was one main street. I remember when my grandmother came to visit me. She came in to tell us that she had won the lottery. She was able to able to buy a chicken for my birthday, and that was really an important thing. It was a big experience in her life because she did not win the lottery that often. It was 8 of out 10 points, and that was really good.

This was when you were born?

This was when I was born, because my parents were very poor. My father did not have a city job. My father was a graduate of Stanford University and could not get a job. Standard Oil gave him a part-time, temporary job. They were poor because they had to support his family—my aunt and her son—because my uncle had died overseas. He was the first pilot in the air force in China. He was looking for airfields for Chiang Kai Shek.

So your dad had a temporary job and he was supporting his parents. Were they living with you?

No, at that time they were still living in San Jose. They didn't come down to Whittier until after my mother opened up her store, I think. I remember when they came down. It was very exciting; my parents had bought new furniture for them.

And they moved in with you?

Of course.

Tell me about your mom's store. When did she do that? How did she come to open a store?

They were very poor. I was a sickly child because I was malnourished when I was born. My father did not like avocados even though they're considered a delicacy now. He had to eat avocado sandwiches every day [because they were cheap], and he resented that.

What was it like growing up in Whittier? What was Whittier like? I know that you said that it was a one-horse town, but what were the people like?

It was a Quaker town. It was a suburb of Los Angeles at the time, but we were the only Chinese in town. There was a Japanese family who ran a farm and sold produce. There was also a Korean who sold produce and we ran into him and his wife afterwards when I was a systems engineer [at Bell Labs] and we were having crabs. [. . .] We met them, and he was from Whittier! I said, how interesting; that's where I was born!

Now as I understand, it was a Quaker town with a lot of retired missionaries. Is that right?

Yes, the missionaries were constantly getting us to go to church—their church, of course. There was a church on every corner of every block. But my mother was Catholic, and she made sure that we attended every denomination in San Francisco, but I didn't miss my religion.

When did you move up to San Francisco? What made you decide to move up to San Francisco?

Let me just finish Whittier.

Sure, please.

Whittier was a one-horse town. There were Quakers who lived there; it was primarily a Quaker city, and there were missionaries who had come back from China. My mother was a darling among these people. They would invite her to tea, because she was an exotic doll. I remember when my sister was born three and a half years after I was, and she was cute. Connie. She was so cute. We had a bassinet; it was so frilly and so beautiful. I didn't know that babies were messy at that time. But I just remember that she was so very cute.

That was Connie.

There were two girls, and my father was called overseas after World

War II [began]. My mother was very upset because she had just opened up her store. She didn't know very much English and she felt that she couldn't handle the store and his being away. My grandpa came and helped her at the store. I remember Grandpa. He was always a gentleman, and he was really lovable.

That grandpa was your dad's dad?

Yes, my father's side.

The one who ran a grocery store in San Jose?

Yes, he came down from San Jose to help my mother. She thought of opening up a store. It came to her when she was wheeling me around town. She thought that she could open up a gift shop. She had never done anything [like that] before in her life, but she ran the gift shop. I remember sitting in the depot waiting for her. I would be guarding the merchandise, and she would be buying the tickets or whatever to take us back home. That was when we would take the train or bus back from San Francisco. Her mother was in San Francisco, and my mother was the darling.

That was your mom. One of the important things about your story is that you've done so many things. Especially your career, because you started out and went to Stanford, right?

Yes,

And you did your degree in . . .

Microbiology.

And then you went on?

In those days it was very different. It was before the women's lib movement. We were all expected to get pinned. We were being pinned; it was very important. You became engaged and then got married. That was it! That was the whole essence of being a woman. My father was adamant that his daughters would go to college even though college was difficult for us [financially]. I couldn't find a suitable major that would make my mother happy. She was always worried that I wouldn't find a husband. The only reason I went to college was because my father thought otherwise. But he was very open for his age.

Now your career took some major turns for women of your generation. Your major at Stanford was medical microbiology and then you ended up getting your doctorate in education and psychology. How did that happen?

Well medical microbiology was an acceptable career for my mother. Because if I were a doctor or lawyer, no men would see me or take me out. So she was determined that I get my MRS degree before I left college. Then you came along.

Then I came along. Your mother roped me in. Then after you got out of Stanford, you did something in public health.

Well I was just a public health . . . what did they call it?

You were certified in public health or something. And then we got married and moved up to Oregon. You continued your science track. But then at some point you turned towards psychology and education. What was it that turned you that way?

You wanted to go to [med] school and you said that education was the only thing that I could do. I had to support you.

But at one point you were thinking of genetics for your doctorate, weren't you?

No, I wasn't. It was primarily to put you through school. So I went for my education degree, and in the meantime I couldn't find a thesis topic. I gravitated towards psychology. My mother had been very adamant that I not major in psychology because she believed that no one would marry me.

She was very focused on you getting your MRS degree, wasn't she?

She was. I remember reading [Emily Post's etiquette] book on what you and I were supposed to do.

When you got into education and into psychology, how rough was it getting your doctorate? How hard was it? . . . You were working then, too?

No, at that time women who went to school were frowned upon. I had three boys then. They were about a year and a half apart. I had to find a babysitter for Lloyd. I was feeling very guilty because you can't leave a child with anyone. One of our neighbors was good enough to take him on.

I was kind of thinking that when you were getting your EdD, that you were working full-time.

And going skiing.

Now how did you get the boys into skiing? That's not something that Asian Americans got into in that era.

I was determined that my boys would learn to ski. We were in Minneapolis. We had gotten married and moved to Oregon. The two boys were born in Oregon and you then went to school in Chicago. We were in a three-story walkup, and I remember my dad crying when he first saw the conditions that I lived in. It was a walkup, three stories, and there was a dirt floor in the basement. Well, Chicago was really terrible looking at that time. The rickety stairs. . . . I had two in diapers, and I didn't work at that time. I didn't go to school. We moved from Oregon to Chicago, and then Chicago to St. Louis, St. Louis to Minneapolis, and then Minneapolis to New Jersey. That was a good move, because we bought a house.

So you said that you got interested in getting the boys into skiing in Minneapolis?

Yes, I was remembering that I had to take the boys skiing, but it was too costly and I couldn't afford it. I was determined that they would go skiing. So when I got to New Jersey—after you moved from General Mills to the ad agency—that's when I met Mrs. Bruzzio [a neighbor]. Her children were older and they had skis. So I was able to borrow them.

I remember when you taught them by putting them between [your legs]. They used to use the old rope tows. You put the kids between your legs to get them up the hill?

No, they were really good. They did it all by themselves.

Even the youngest one?

Even the youngest one.

So that's how you got into skiing, and the boys are great skiers.

Yes, they're all right.

Because of you and Mrs. Bruzzio. You became a very fast skier yourself.

I liked to ski. I remember the first time. The first time it snowed in Somerset, I bundled up the boys. Elliott was the first one I took skiing because he was so good. I remember that he was following all the steps that the instructor told us and was watching everything that we did and could copy it. So he became a good skier, because he liked to follow directions. Lloyd had lessons too. You made a rope tow for the boys.

Yes, the rope tow inside the house. I was the motor, so we could practice getting on the rope tow.

But I had injured myself during the first season that we went skiing because I was so anxious for them to ski that I fell on the rope tow. That was when I hurt my knee. After that the boys were natural skiers.

What about Dwight?

He was a natural. He was very good.

Do you remember when he skied backwards so that he could talk to us? He was ten or twelve years old?

Ten. I'd like to go back to when I was director of the [Institute for] Science, Technology and Society [at Rutgers] and I constructed a curriculum [on environmental issues for K through 12 students based on] Kohlberg's stages.[43] . . .

The institute was at Rutgers?

Yes, that was when we were in Somerset, New Jersey.

You used to travel around the state a lot. What were you doing then? Was that related to the curriculum?

---

43 Psychologist Lawrence Kohlberg's six stages of development of moral reasoning. Janey's curriculum used different environmental dilemma stories that students had to resolve.

Yes it was. . . . We were involved in the environment and it was the Center for Environmental and Coastal Studies. We were housed there, but we were independent of them. We had a grant that allowed us to develop the curriculum. I developed the curriculum for K through 12, and that required me to travel to different places in New Jersey, because we were looking for schools that would test the curriculum, field-test it. We went to Rumson and Red Bank. Rumson also asked us to field test the curriculum. It was based on Kohlberg's model of moral reasoning. That took me to different places in New Jersey.

That must have been very unusual for most schools at the time.

Yes, it was. It was really based on short stories that had a moral dilemma to them. I felt that the short stories needed more than just a story; they needed facts to back up their arguments. They had to extract facts from the reading that they could use. It was based on data, and we provided the data that they needed. That was the curriculum. The important thing was the questions that would [prompt] them to talk about their dilemmas. These dilemmas were focused on food, the environment, bioethics, and conservation.

And so to engage the students you used the dilemma to pose a problem and see how they would come to a solution?

Yes, or how they would decide on which way to go. The teachers were amazed at [how well their students understood environmental dilemmas] when they would try these modules, which were based on Kohlbergian theory. Kohlberg was a follower of Piaget. That's how I got into the Piagetian theories of child development.

Which is what you used in your thesis?

No, it was entirely different.

The Kohlberg model was what you used for your curriculum development, which was different than your thesis.

The Kohlberg model . . . was approved by the government, which was not supportive of anything to do with moral reasoning. It was the Reagan administration that put a damper on our funding. The funding was cut off, and we couldn't do anything more, so the curriculum was totally defunct.

What a shame. It is very interesting to think about your career in different steps. You received your doctorate, and then you ended up at Bell Laboratories.

The person at Bell Labs said that I shouldn't apply until I finished my doctorate. So I had to finish my doctorate. I didn't know how to finish it. The writing of it was most difficult, for me.

In what way was it the most difficult?

It was because I had to write a thesis. Writing was always difficult for me. That's why I went to the sciences, because I thought I wouldn't have to write or read. Or to speak. So I avoided anything that had to do with English, and chose the sciences thinking that I wouldn't have to deal with any of that. It's not true, because everything I did afterwards was related to writing and verbalizing. I realized that it was really a mistake on my part.

By the time you retired from Bell Labs, you could give impromptu talks and write easily. What brought about that change?

Because I felt that I had to do that, because it was expected of me. That was my job. My job was to expound on theory. I had to convince other people that it was important and that I was right. So I had to do whatever I could to change other people's viewpoints.

You were in a very specialized area of telecommunications, as a system engineer, weren't you? I remember meeting one of your colleagues using the same phrase that you used for dummies like us ordinary people, saying that "we're the ding-a-ling" of the telephone. What did you mean by that? Why was this phrase used to explain the work done by your signaling unit?

I worked on the "ding-a-ling" system of the telephone.

What does that mean?

It means that I worked on the protocols, the handshake between people—the "ding-a-ling."

When one connects to another, there's some sort of electronic handshake between systems. Is that what it is?

No, it was handshake between different protocols. That was what we talked about.

That was a very esoteric group that went to Geneva. You went to Geneva a lot. What were you doing there? How often did you go?

Twice a year, for two weeks.

You were part of the United Nations over there. What were you doing?

We refined the protocol,[44] because we had to have agreement between all the nations before it was finalized. We focused on getting agreements with different countries, so we had to meet in Geneva. It was held at the United Nations building. It was the UN headquarters—the League of Nations, which became the UN. It was the League of Nations building. We had lunch over there, the older building. Then we had the newer building, which was part of the new development.

Your colleagues really liked being with you after the meetings? Why was that?

Because I would lead them to restaurants. They liked the restaurants that I selected. That's because I had three boys who liked to eat, and I spent my time cooking for them. Every day it was something different, and I had to build my repertoire of cooking skills. So I knew restaurants very well.

Did your passion for food have anything to do with the fact that your dad was a partner in two restaurants?

No, I thought it was independent of that. The restaurants put me through school. Though he was a partner in restaurants, that was when he came up to San Francisco. He had to be a soy sauce man, it was a family business. When he came back from World War II, he joined our family business in San Francisco. That was the reason we

---

44 The protocol for transmitting telephone calls between national telephone systems.

moved to San Francisco from Whittier. My mother's gift shop was quite a success, and then we moved to San Francisco. We lived in an apartment for a year. My mother was very upset, because it was a one-bedroom apartment for five of us. She and my dad slept on the couch, and then the three children had the bedroom. By that time there was my brother who came right after my father came back from the war. There were two girls and one little boy, all in one little apartment, which was subleased from my uncle. My uncle subleased it to us, but he disappeared because he was a gambler.

There's an interesting trend, because there's a passion for food and knowing about restaurants. And it's come together because of your volunteering. Can you tell us about that? Can you tell me about your volunteering at the New York Public Library and how it's gotten you involved in food and restaurants?

Joan McCann told me that the library was good for volunteering, so I decided to look it up. It was all by accident.

Do you enjoy it?

It was like the time that I went to Oregon Medical School looking for a job. They said, "Why look for a job when you can go to school and we'll pay you?" So I went to school and received pay as well. But I remember that I made more than you did!

Your scholarship was bigger than mine?

Yes, ten dollars more.

But together we had a pretty good life, didn't we?

Yes, it was good. It was tax free, and taxes were one-third to one-half [of salaries].

We just got back from Montreal two weeks ago.

We spent our 50th anniversary there.

Yes, we spent our 50th anniversary courtesy of the boys. Fifty years of marriage! Someone recently said to me that only six percent of marriages make it to the 50th year. What's your feeling about that? What's it been like to have been married 50 years?

I think that it went too fast. It was much too fast. It went so fast because I had three boys before I could say boo. The three boys kept me very busy. In fact, I didn't have any time to participate in any of the rabble rousing that was going on. That was when my sister was very active in denigrating the war [in Vietnam].

She was very involved in politics?

Yes she was, but I didn't have time to even read the paper. All I remember was that I had to wash two pails of diapers every day.

As I remember it, you were able to combine your passion for cooking with politics. Remember the fellow John Anderson who was running as an independent for president? You cooked that fantastic meal by yourself for 50 people, while everyone stood by waiting for you to serve it. That was quite an accomplishment.

Yes it was.

How did you get such a level of skill that you could cook for 50 people?

I just tripled the portions, or multiplied by whatever I had. Since I cooked for five, I made ten times more.

That was quite an achievement, cooking wise. Now you continue to serve as Alexandra's guide to restaurants every week.

Yes, that's a person I met through the library. She was looking for someone to go to the opera with. She was so glad that I had an apartment in the same building. She doesn't cook at all, so she depends on me to find restaurants.

Looking back on a fantastic career and 50 years of marriage, what are some of the highlights of your career?

You and the boys.

Janey's "Autobiography" in her Stanford Class Reunion Book

Janey used her personal page in the Stanford Class of 1960's 50th class reunion book to share her life story with her classmates. She had been diagnosed with a terminal brain disease several years earlier and by the time of the class reunion in 2010 was experiencing symptoms affecting her mobility, dexterity, and speech, but she had no loss of mental capability. The comments and information she provided for the class reunion book complement what she said in her StoryCorps interview the following year. This is how she remembered Stanford and her life:

Stanford Memories
Saturday mornings in English and Western Civ classes.
Lab in Chem. Building on Friday afternoons.
Dressing for dinner on Sundays.
Rushing for Mass on Sundays at St. Ann in Palo Alto.
Long-stemmed roses from Richard after being pinned.

Career
California State Public Health Microbiologist
Graduate Student (Microbiology) U. of Oregon Med. School
Biology Teacher, Duschesne High School, St. Charles, MO
Ed.D.—Psychology & Education, Rutgers University
Curriculum Designer, Rutgers University
Systems Engineer, Bell Laboratories, Holmdel, NJ

Volunteer
New York Public Library, Main Branch, New York City
Mount Vernon Hotel Museum, New York City
National Park Service/Amtrak, volunteer, Trails & Rails program

Places I've Been
My work at Bell Laboratories included extensive international travel, which allowed me to visit many countries in Western Europe and Asia, including Switzerland, France, Germany, Italy, Great Britain, Singapore, and Japan. Personal travel with Stanford friends and husband took me to Austria, China, Hong Kong, Taiwan, Thailand, Mexico, Spain, Portugal, Morocco, and Canada.

Lived in Portland, OR, Chicago, IL, St. Louis, MO, Minneapolis, MN, Central New Jersey, Jersey Shore, Jersey City, NJ, and (finally) Manhattan, NY.

In Memoriam
Janey Young Cheu
August 20, 1938–May 31, 2015